WAKE UP...
LIVE THE LIFE YOU LOVE

LIVING IN ABUNDANCE

Wake Up... Live the Life You Love
Living in Abundance

Little Seed Publishing
Laguna Beach, CA

Pre-Press Management by New Caledonian Press
Text Design: Angie Kimbro

Cover Design and Illustrations: K-Squared Designs, LLC, www.k2ds.com
Publisher intends this material for entertainment and no legal, medical or other
professional advice is implied or expressed. If the purchaser cannot abide by this
statement, please return the book for a full refund.

Acknowledgement is made for permission to quote copyrighted materials.

For information, contact Little Seed Publishing's operations office at Global
Partnership: P.O. Box 894, Murray, KY 42071 or phone 270-753-5225 (CST).

Distributed by Global Partnership, LLC
608-B Main Street
Murray, KY 42071

Library of Congress Cataloguing In Publication Data
Wake Up... Live the Life You Love: Living In Abundance
ISBN-10: 1-933063-09-2
ISBN-13: 978-1-933063-09-6

$14.95 USA $14.95 Canada

Other books by Steven E, and Lee Beard

Wake Up...Live the Life You Love:
...First Edition
...Second Edition
...Inspirational How-to Stories
...In Beauty
...Living on Purpose
...Finding Your Life's Passion
...Purpose, Passion, Abundance
...Finding Personal Freedom
...Seizing Your Success
...Giving Gratitude
...On the Enlightened Path
...In Spirit
...Finding Life's Passion
...Stories of Transformation
...A Search for Purpose

Wake Up...Shape Up...Live the Life You Love

How would you like to be in the next book with a fabulous group of best-selling authors? Another Wake Up book is coming soon!

Visit: WakeUpLive.com

We would like to provide you with a free gift to enhance this book experience.

For your free gift, please visit: WakeUpGift.com.

TABLE OF CONTENTS

LIVING IN ABUNDANCE

LIVING IN ABUNDANCE

FOREWORD

"We can't all be rich; we can't all be happy."

So many people believe that the world is a small, limited and limiting place. Other people seem to have cornered the market on happiness, or money, or fulfillment, so there is little or nothing left for those whose dreams are not already reality. They work hard and do great things, but they don't believe that a true sense of fulfillment is available to them.

This book contains the words and the wishes of those who are out to change that imprisoning view of life. There are lessons you can learn from them; there are plans of action that may bring you to the understanding that abundance can be yours.

Steven E is approaching the 25th book in the series that has made him internationally renowned; his last three books are being translated for sale in China. Years ago, he was drifting from job to job, sleeping on friends' couches and living in his car. Then, with the help of extensive reading and an inspirational dream, he began his career as a motivational speaker, writer and organizer.

We expected a number of essays about wealth, money, position and power. I don't think any of us expected to be overwhelmed by the stories of giving; of withdrawal from power in preference for family; of finding joy in service. Even the tales of those who found wealth and fame argue that family and sharing are the only true avenues to abundance. It's been truly inspiring.

 *Robert Valentine, Senior Editor*

WAKE UP...
LIVE THE LIFE YOU LOVE

LIVING IN
ABUNDANCE

BEING GRATEFUL FOR NOW
Steven E

We seem to get caught up in living in either the past or the future. We need to focus on the present moment. When we keep our power in the present, we become more attuned to our life and our surroundings.

The next time you are washing the dishes, watch the water come out of the faucet and the bubbles rise in the water. Pay attention to your hands washing the dishes. Absorb yourself in the moment and not on how you will maneuver tomorrow.

Start being aware of your thoughts. Your intentions create the reality you are living. Until you become aware of this, it happens unconsciously. Now, close your eyes and picture your current life situation—your relationships, finances, job and family.

Open your eyes. Find yourself in the moment and know that you have created your whole life consciously or unconsciously. Live your life in the present and **create the life that you love**. It is so easy to be grateful for the simple beauty; the common miracle of your life right now.

At birth, your subconscious mind began to record your every feeling, thought and word, and you accepted whatever your parents and teachers told you. Those who taught you their beliefs probably loved you dearly and did the very best they could. You learned their ways, their weaknesses and limitations, their fears, self-guilt and sins, along with the positive messages they tried to relay to you.

I realized that 95 percent of what I learned as a child was the limitations of other people; we hold onto many of these beliefs about self-worth, our body, our attractiveness, our goodness and our finances. All these beliefs came from somewhere. NOW, they are our reality; they are the truth about you, and you hold onto them very tightly.

LIVING IN ABUNDANCE

What we believe creates our world and our reality. Now is the time to leave behind all your old self-defeating and destructive beliefs. Get rid of them! Listen to your own heart. Learn to forgive yourself and realize that we punish ourselves for our so-called sins. Realize that sin is self-inflicted nonsense. Forgive yourself; thank yourself; love yourself.

We become the way we think of and feel about ourselves. If we think from fear and limitation, we imprison ourselves. When we learn to sit quietly and go within, we find our true self and discover peace; we find our true, free and loving spirit.

This process will rid us of our old negative beliefs. This freedom will take us beyond mass thinking, which is programmed by fear and limitation. When we listen to our inner selves, we will live a life that we love, and we will live it in the now.

 Steven E

IT'S ABOUT US
Margaret L. Good

Why are we here? What is the purpose of life? I have asked myself these questions many, many times and, though the answer may be different for each of us, I believe the fundamental principles are the same. When I put those principles into practice, I found my life flourished, all my needs were met and I could live with inner peace—free from worry. I am free from worry because all of my needs have been, and will continue to be, met. I realized needs are different from wants. Do I need a Mercedes to get the job done, or will a Ford Focus do? This, too, is an individual question, dependent upon your own circumstances. What is important to recognize is that if you need the Mercedes to accomplish your mission here on earth, a Mercedes or its equivalent will be provided.

So why are we here and what is life about? When I realized that everything we have on earth is a gift to us and we are stewards of these gifts, my life changed. Realizing that life is not all about me caused me to change my attitude toward others. No man is an island. Like the different parts of our bodies, which have different functions, we are all different. We are precious gifts to each other, and we need each other if we are going to enjoy this life to its fullest and reach our potential. We have been entrusted with all of the world's resources and are accountable for what we do with them.

So, how do we treat a precious gift? Let's use a pet or baby as an example. We treat them with love, kindness, goodness, joy, peace, patience, faithfulness, gentleness and self-control. We show them care and compassion. We show them hope and respect. So why do we change this behavior toward each other and ourselves as we grow older?

After having an abusive boss, an unethical business partner and a life filled with unmet goals, I decided to treat everyone I meet as a precious gift to me. Initially it was a struggle. We can expect conflict and strife. We live in an imperfect and incomplete world and it can be frustrating—reality often falls short of ideal. Knowing that the enemy prowls around us each day like a roaring lion looking for someone to devour, it takes a lot of energy to be self-controlled and alert. Like a runner in a race, our life up to this date has been a training ground for the future. We must handle each new situation by looking forward and using the good things from the past to propel us to the finish line. If we focus on the past, like a runner looking over his shoulder at the runner behind him, we will stumble, fall and lose the race.

We spend 40 percent of our waking hours at work, and work is a noble thing—thus, it is important for it to be meaningful. After my businesses failed, I had to regroup and start over. As an accountant, I needed my practice to grow again, but I wanted to work with the right people. I realized that one of my gifts was taking a client's dreams and goals, putting together an action plan and helping them carry out the implementation process to see their business grow. Being a doer was a gift.

To reach these goals, it was important to hire the right people. This requires wisdom and discernment. Today the personal touch is gone. My business began around the New Year, so for my first marketing effort, I purchased 250 calendars that had a space to put my business card. I hand-wrote a note to each business owner, letting them know I wished them a great year in business and that I was available to help them reach their goals—whatever that meant for them.

I interviewed the potential clients and suppliers to ensure that the people I dealt with had the same values and principles as I did. I asked them about their attitudes toward life, as well as their values, beliefs and goals. I also asked about their philosophies and definitions of the golden rule. I worked only with those who wanted to make a contribution to others, who put their focus on how to better the lives of others and who realized that life is not about them, but about "us;" it's about helping each other reach our full potential in all areas of life. When your heart is in the right place, amazing things happen. I had to stop sending out my calendars after the first 40; the response was more than I could handle.

It is important to be strong and courageous, and to be careful to obey all the laws if you want to be successful. People want to do business with those who are honest and who have integrity. Having a team that is trustworthy and dependable enhances the clients' confidence in you. When people know they can count on you, especially when they are in need and under pressure, your value increases, business soars and more opportunities arise than you can imagine. When people are your top priority and you recognize them for their valued contribution, they will remain loyal to you. When you see others as an extension of yourself and treat them with respect, fairness and understanding—instead of as a means to an end—they will become motivated to be the best they can be. They will come to work happy, motivated, fulfilled and ready to optimize their potential. They will be eager, will work vigorously and will pursue excellence. Through love and compassion, I have been able to show clients that respect, fairness and understanding. I am also able to be sensitive, determine their needs and be responsive to them.

Realizing that each of us is a precious gift and treating everyone in that manner was the key to a fulfilling life at home, work and play. It has also brought many opportunities into my life. Partnering with those of noble character and realizing that the world is abundant enough to meet our needs has opened more doors for me than I could have ever imagined.

 *Margaret L. Good*

BE FREE TO FEEL THE ABUNDANCE
Kayli Martin & Donna Lee Cutler

<u>Be</u>
When you multi-task
You are moving way too fast
So instead, slip into **Slow**
Give yourself permission
Do nothing but **listen**
And you might
Feel humor and joy
And find
Time to **be**.

Bold, shocking headlines greet us every morning. Broadcasters regurgitate sensational news. Advertisers create artificial needs that can only be filled with their products. We are constantly bombarded with negativity. Ask yourself one simple question: How do I feel when I hear the negative details in the news or the constant "buy me" demands from advertisers?

The relentless exposure to stories of violence and to advertisers' demands can lead to feelings of numbness and distress, which reflect negative stress overload. This way of living is not inevitable. If you wake up and become aware of the possibility of enjoying a simpler, more positive approach to life and have an appreciation for the elegant natural beauty all around, you can find joy and gratitude for new beginnings every day.

Donna's story:
About two years ago, I came down with bronchitis. I ignored my body and continued at my normal pace: operating a business and caring for my family's needs. Eventually, I developed walking pneumonia that

hung on for months. I realized my body was yelling for me to *"WAKE UP!"* But instead of responding to my body's needs, I took the route of self-criticism, "what if" situations, self-doubt and depression. After spending several months in this state, I came to the conclusion that I needed to get back in control of myself. However, I made a very common mistake—the mistake of adding to my already hectic life. I scheduled time to exercise at the gym and to participate in a daily Yoga program. On top of that, I revamped my diet, adding yet another layer of stress.

During this same period, my elderly parents, who lived in another state, became fragile and required additional assistance in order to continue living in their own home. Thus, I added to my list frequent travel and time away from my business and family to assist my parents. I kept adding things to my schedule, but never felt that I could remove any of my commitments. I became increasingly automatic and numb to all that I was doing. On one occasion toward the end of my dad's life, he commented, "I don't have much time on this earth. I wish I was 20 years younger." At that moment, I clearly heard, *"WAKE UP—what is truly important here? Where is the love, joy and passion?"*

As far back as I can remember, I have always had a lot of energy. Being positive is part of who I am. My life is full of things I enjoy doing. Because I have many tasks I need to accomplish each day, I have learned to multi-task. But I have also learned to stop, sit, listen and just *be*. I get up early to watch and listen to the natural world waking up. Writing poetry has been an added expression of this daily joyful experience.

My conversations have a common beginning: "How are you doing?" Instead of answering that, I would rather answer the question, "How are you being?" I answer how I am being with a more enthusiastic response. "I am *feeling* in love and passionate. I am *feeling* deeply appreciative of my relationships with my husband and son. I am feeling positive about my work focus and associates. I am feeling peaceful in my living and work environments. I wake up early in the morning feeling enthusiasm, rather than mentally ticking off items in my to-do list for the day." Wouldn't it be a powerful change if everyone took the time to listen, communicate and express their true *being*?

Kayli's story:
I grew up with physical challenges that made it difficult to keep up with typical schedules. Rather than adjusting my expectations of myself accordingly, I forced myself to do more than other people did, to prove to myself that I was just as worthy as they were. One of my college professors told me I had accomplished more than any other student, despite being a single parent and having physical challenges.

By the time I finished my undergraduate work, I had completely exhausted myself, landing in bed for a year of rest. Did I learn my lesson? Not at all. I started graduate school and dove in whole-heartedly because I needed to prove my worthiness to myself. One master's degree and six years of full-time work in the corporate world later, I found myself again utterly fatigued and unable to continue.

This time, I *"WOKE UP!"* I decided that I was no longer going to try to keep up with other people. I was going to focus on being and playing. I deliberately chose to think about positive things because ". . .whatsoever things are true. . .whatsoever things are pure, whatsoever things are lovely, whatsoever things are of good report; if there be any virtue. . .think on these things." (Philippians 4:8, KJV) Many religions say that what you send out comes back to you. I found this to be true.

As I focused my thoughts and choices in more positive directions, positive things began happening in my life. Four years ago, Donna and I met, connecting in ways we are still discovering. We started a business together that has prospered each year. Now, we divide our time between tending to our business and expressing our creativity through poetry, writing and music.

LIVING IN ABUNDANCE

Slowing down, listening to ourselves and allowing ourselves to be has dramatically changed both our lives for the better. Instead of worrying over endless to-do lists, we plan our week including time to care for ourselves, our business, our clients and our play times. We actively seek ways to incorporate more joy and laughter in our lives.

There are many opportunities for making choices that affect your life positively or negatively. When you are numb and overwhelmed, it is difficult to know what you're feeling, to realize how the choices you make affect you, or even to comprehend that you are constantly making choices. The challenge is to *"Wake Up!"* and become aware of what you are feeling here and now. By slowing down, listening to yourself and allowing yourself to be, you can make choices consciously. You can fall in love with the life you are creating.

Kayli Martin & Donna Lee Cutler

NETWORK YOUR WAY TO ALL OF THE ABUNDANCE YOU DESERVE
James Malinchak

Why is networking important for creating all of the abundance you deserve? The answer is simple. It's not a coincidence that hundreds, even thousands, of people are hired for positions over individuals who are more qualified and more experienced merely because they have cultivated relationships with key centers of influence. It's not a coincidence when one politician is elected into office over another because he has cultivated relationships with more individual voters than the opposition. Through networking you will receive opportunities that will expand your current knowledge base. Through networking you will be put in positions to expand your current skills and learn to communicate at many levels.

Networking is communicating with others to create mutually beneficial relationships.

People often confuse networking with "quantity of contracts." However, the purpose of networking is simply to enhance your cause. Think of networking as the opening of doors to the unknown. You might be tempted to believe the more doors you have, the greater the odds you will make the right kinds of connections, but that is incorrect. Networking is intentional by design. By placing yourself in situations that attract others with whom mutually beneficial relationships can be established, you increase the potential payoffs. Therefore, one of the greatest traits of the networking leader is the ability to actively identify which doors to open.

Networking Development Tips

Tip No. 1 – Do Your Homework
Because planning is a component of networking, you will need to make

lists and seek out resources that can answer basic questions about the person or organization you will be meeting. For instance, who knows the person you are trying to meet? Who else works with this person? Where do they live? I'm not suggesting you stalk your potential pool of networking targets; rather, sit down and list the information that might help increase the quality of your potential interactions.

I learned the importance of doing your homework when I had the opportunity to have dinner with author Mary Higgins Clark. Despite the many possible ways of learning more about my famous upcoming dinner host, time required that I select only a few. Step one was a trip to my local bookstore—a place of great networking resources. I asked the person working behind the counter if she had ever heard of Mary Higgins Clark. "Oh yes," she replied, as she pointed to a display holding more than 10 of her books. Now I felt anxious; despite my desire to read what appeared to be stacks upon stacks of her best-selling novels, I purchased only three to read on the plane. As I left the bookstore, I found myself less anxious and more excited about my upcoming encounter.

Tip No. 2 – Take the Initiative and Introduce Yourself
When meeting someone of notoriety, it is natural to be nervous about making a bad first impression, regardless of your own level of success. Even the most charismatic individuals say the wrong things out of nervousness or excitement. I think it's always wise to rely on politeness. This seems like an obvious suggestion until you mistakenly call someone by her first name after a two-minute introduction. Whether the person you are approaching is famous or not, it's always acceptable to ask, "How would you like to be addressed?" after introducing yourself. I also like to have a few questions in mind that begin with the phrase, "Tell me about…," followed by a reference to something I know about the person. Because most people like to talk about themselves, the more the conversation places emphasis on your new acquaintance—not why they should be thrilled to meet you—the more likely will be another encounter.

Fortunately, I didn't have to make any decisions about how to approach my dinner host since Mary Higgins Clark greeted me as I approached her home. Still outside, Mary and I talked about a host of topics, from our families and hobbies to the stock market. She was very interested in the market. She asked questions that, frankly, were rather complicated to answer. Instead of trying to impress her (a mistake often made when trying to make a good impression), I responded to her questions with simple, easy-to-understand answers.

Tip No. 3 – Make it About Them
You never want to try to make yourself sound better, smarter or more knowledgeable than your partners in conversation. When you do this, you appear condescending and, despite your desire to build a foundation for additional interaction, you may have just closed the door. In fact, it should be your goal to ask more questions than you answer. Keep the other person engaged in the conversation by having them share information about themselves. Find a common interest. Last, do what is needed to make yourself appear approachable. Offering your business card is just one way to ensure this happens.

Much to my delight, my use of effective networking skills with Mary Higgins Clark was immediately rewarded. For example, as I was leaving after a wonderful evening of conversation over a New England dinner, Mary asked if she could talk to me for a minute. I walked with her to the corner of the room where she said, "I really like you and how easily you explained the answers to my questions. I'm looking to open an investment account with another company, and I'd like to open the account with you."

Tip No. 4 – Stay in Frequent Contact
Why did this happen? Simply because I took the initiative to stay in contact and follow up with her. There are many ways you can do this. Writing thank you cards, sending articles of interest with a note or remembering events of significance with flowers are all examples of frequent contact. Sending an e-mail message—although impersonal when

compared to a letter—also keeps your name and contact information out there. Call certain contacts periodically and, if you happen to be in their area, take them to lunch or give them a quick call to say hello.

Tip No. 5 – Look for Ways to Offer Praise

Making others feel good is essential for walking through doors once they have been opened. Congratulating someone for accomplishments or thanking them for taking the time to speak with you are ways to praise. This does not mean you should act like a crazed fan; rather, think about what you could say that would make the other person feel good about themselves. Praising your own accomplishments can lead to a competitive tone in your conversations. Having a calm sense of self while praising others makes you appear self-confident and much more worthy of additional contacts.

A Child Speaks Volumes

I was speaking in San Antonio, where my cousin Davy lives. It had been several years since we had seen each other. Therefore, the invitation to stay at his house rather than in a hotel was warmly received.

The night of my talk, Davy asked if he could bring his 9-year-old son, Kevin, because he wanted to begin exposing him to things that could be helpful to his future success. Naturally, I agreed. However, I mentioned that Kevin probably wouldn't be able to relate to most of the information. Davy understood, but wanted his son to attend nonetheless.

For about 90 minutes, I spoke about how to create a powerful network of contacts. I emphasized the importance of making others feel good about themselves. Among the variety of suggestions was simply to take the time to leave a note for someone praising them for something they did that day.

After the talk, Davy, Kevin and I stayed another hour and a half so I could answer questions and autograph books. It was now about 11 p.m.

and past Kevin's bedtime. As a matter of fact, I noticed that Kevin was sleeping while I was answering questions and signing books. He continued to sleep on the ride home and as Davy and I took him to his bedroom.

The next morning, I got out of bed and prepared to take a shower. As I opened the bedroom door, something caught my eye. A note with my name on it was taped to the door. It said, *"Dear Cousin James, I just wanted to let you know that you did great last night. I can't wait to see you when I get home from school. Love, Kevin."* Wow! I couldn't believe it! Kevin's simple gesture made me feel great and motivated me to make an effort to leave more notes for others. If a 9-year-old can take such initiative to praise, grown leaders can certainly do the same.

Final Words
No successful person achieves goals without the assistance of others. It doesn't matter how knowledgeable, qualified or experienced you are: Without the assistance of others, you will probably fail to excel. Push yourself to stretch outside your immediate comfort zone; seek different ideas and discover a world of potential opportunities for yourself and your organization.

Mastering the art of networking will enhance your abilities and opportunities to create all of the abundance you deserve!

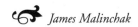 *James Malinchak*

BECAUSE OF ONE
Mike Hayashi

Freshman year, sitting on the sofa in my college dorm lobby at 11 p.m., patiently anticipating that first kiss on our very first date. I watched her casually reach deep into her purse....

The next few moments seemed surreal to me as she calmly held a six-inch switchblade just under my right eye and told me no man was ever going to touch her and treat her like a piece of garbage ever again. "Do we understand each other?" she asked. I can't remember the exact words that came out of my mouth, but I remember nodding my head up and down and saying yes three or four times. Having a blade in my face and looking into her eyes filled with pure anger and frustration made an impression on me that haunts me still. What could anyone have done to her to make her feel the absolute disdain she felt for all men—even me? Why did she feel the urgent need to draw me into her painful past?

She had been violently raped by four young boys when she was only 15 years old. It was no big deal to them. In their sick, young minds, no one really got hurt; and as our judicial system often allows, these teenagers were never arrested or convicted of a crime. Why did she assume that I had no respect for her and that I had the same insensitive, cruel and disgusting views of women as those who committed these horrific acts against her three years before? Why was she willing to take the chance of scaring me off so early in our relationship? It seemed unfair to me that I was being persecuted for the crimes of another, but I sat perfectly still and listened to her as I have never listened to any other woman in my life. She told me her story with the blade still inches from my face.

This first date took three months of preparation. We met while I was playing drums in a small jazz trio at a country club where she worked as a waitress on weekends. The day was picture-perfect from the first moment we were able to hug and hold hands and cuddle that after-noon. As day grew into night and we shared our first meal, the time flew by—I can't even remember the movie we walked across campus to see. I do, however, remember her beautiful, brown eyes, her long, dark hair, her incredible smile and her infectious laugh. Right up to the sec-ond she placed that knife up to my face, I had thought this was the best eight hours I'd ever spent with anyone.

As a freshman in college, I didn't have the words, the knowledge, the creativity or even a clue how to respond to her horrifying story. I had two years of Karate behind me, but nothing to relate to her with—no comforting words or counseling skills. She was my first exposure to the word "rape" and how a survivor copes with this insidious crime. Her family had swept it under the carpet of shame. "Don't talk about it," they had said. "At least they didn't really hurt you." Family embarrass-ment, cultural perspectives, fear of reliving that nightmare through the media and the eyes of the law seemed as disabling as the crime itself. Her only defense mechanism, besides carrying that blade, was to host a deep disdain, fear and distrust of men—including me. My initial shock never really subsided over the next two days, and I found myself sleep-ing with one eye open both nights, as she lay in my roommate's bed across the room. There was no intimate, physical contact that weekend, even though I may have wanted it.

After that weekend, we made a few more phone calls to each other and wrote a few more letters, but we slowly drifted apart. She really needed professional therapy, guidance and time to heal. Her anger with those who had hurt her kept her from allowing me—and probably any other man—into her life without her switchblade and her signature nightmare story. I just couldn't shake the thoughts I had running through my mind—a combination of fear, confusion, helplessness and the ugly, graphic images she had engrained forever in my memory. We never saw each other again, but from her tragedy, I have educated millions of women and given them the tools to prevent, avoid or even stop an assault altogether.

At 17 years old, I didn't know what to say, what to do or how to ease her pain, but she inspired me to start my own company in 1988 with one mission: to end violence against women! Since the first self-defense class I taught (to only 16 women at a local health club), more than 250,000 women at dozens of Fortune 500 Companies, universities, associations, hospitals and churches have participated in my classes in 20 states.

The negative images that haunted my thoughts were the catalysts to organizing the city-wide women's self-defense fundraisers that, for six years, attracted 1,000 to 2,500 women and teenagers annually. From that project, thousands of dollars were donated to women's shelters and rape crisis centers. I also had sessions filmed for cable television, which aired 60 to 70 times each year to more than 2.5 million female viewers. The program was so inspiring, unique and entertaining that it was nominated for an Emmy Award for community service programs in 1994. This media milestone led to the creation of self-defense books, videos, DVDs, and an invitation to be a spokesperson for Taser International, promoting non-lethal personal protection products to female consumers. Most recently, work has begun on a new weekly spot focusing on women's self-defense techniques on a morning television show, reaching another 3.5 million women.

Many women and girls have been spared the trauma of a sexual assault, the horror of domestic violence, the pain and suffering of a physical attack, or the emotional scars of an acquaintance rape because of one violent crime committed against one teenager in a small Midwest town. All the letters, phone calls and e-mails from women, teens and parents of children who have escaped from predators, violent relationships or serial rapists since 1988 validate the education shared with millions of people—all because of one!

Take these thoughts with you and share them:

1) "No" means NO—and you must be able to back up that statement constantly.

2) You may only need self-defense once in your life, but once is enough!

3) One in three women will be a victim of sexual assault. It doesn't have to be you!

4) Violent crimes cost U.S. companies two and a half times an employee's annual salary, but the odds can be reduced with professional, personal safety training.

5) A woman's place is always IN CONTROL.

Take control; share the message. One woman's life led to thousands of lives saved and secured. Because of this one woman, there is an abundance of happiness and confidence.

Because of one.

Mike Hayashi

LIFE WITH A BUNCH OF DUMMIES!
Dr. Keith A. & Cindy C. Robinson

Keith
On April 3, 2003, I was scheduled to autograph copies of my first book, *Growing Older with Your Teeth...Or Something Like Them*. Using humor as a vehicle for teaching public health information to aging people must have struck a note of interest with those at the convention. The lines were long and I quickly became bored with repetitive autographing of books, and I dreamed of escape.

My publicist must have had one of those "sixth sense" moments, as she caught my dreaming eye and rescued me with the words, "Let's take a walk and check out the event for a while." "Happily!" I responded.

As we strolled endless corridors of booths and lines of people, once again my mind began to fog as people began to blend together, becoming an indistinguishable stream of non-descript movement.

That's when it happened. At the time, I had no idea that within a few moments the course of my life would change forever.

As we approached a throng of people who were transfixed by a performance in front of us, they erupted into a burst of laughter, and just as quickly focused again on the sincere message being delivered by the actor. Viewed from the back, this gentleman was dressed in a dark, somewhat baggy, grey suit and a straw hat, and his hand appeared to be lost up the backside of a very large and colorful possum. He was speaking with a British accent, begging the audience for any morsel of chocolate that they might have in their pockets. I made my way into the crowd to partake of the show that was bringing the traffic to a standstill.

With generous doses of "Pardon" and "Excuse me," I made it into the second row, only to find that the man I had viewed from the back was not a man at all. "He" was a "she," and the name printed on her business card read: *Aunt Cindy, nationally recognized ventriloquist and character education specialist.* Breathless, I could only think, "Beautiful, witty, and exceptionally brilliant in her professional delivery of her performance…and her lips didn't move?" After her show, she removed the top hat and a cascade of shimmering, shoulder-length hair fell to its intended place, serving as a perfect frame for the face that I would one day ask to be my wife, literally changing the course of history for both of us.

This view of our first meeting might just be clouded by the storm of hormones erupting deep within this totally unsuspecting, roaming author. In order to be fair and balanced, it might be good to let you see this same meeting from the eyes and heart of Aunt Cindy.

Cindy
April has always been a very special time of year for me. This year, though, I wasn't expecting anything "special" to happen, but it did.

Following my performance with Herschel the Possum, I turned, scanning the crowd for potential clients. That's when my gaze locked on the most inviting, intelligent pair of soft, sweet brown eyes, surrounded by the kindest, most gentle face I'd ever encountered. My heart skipped a few beats and I went over to say hello. After all, maybe this client would be the ticket to several bookings—at least that's what I told myself as I extended my free hand to meet the man responsible for my irregularly beating heart. Since Herschel was still sitting on my hand, I had the perfect vehicle for meeting the owner of those captivating eyes.

It was a scary moment for me since I was now a single mother of two boys and their only means of support. I didn't even consider *dating* to be an option. Once you've had your heart not just broken, but shattered, shredded and shelled out, and survived the healing process, you're not in any hurry to lay it out there for another round of damage!

Besides, I was enjoying coming home to my own room, not having to be at someone else's beck and call, trying to fulfill their demands and expectations. But those eyes drew me in.

As a ventriloquist and character education specialist, I have addressed more than 60,000 students nationwide—words, dummies, voices and accents are the tools of my trade and can be great conversation starters. Herschel the Possum is one of my characters that speaks with a British accent. As I approached the "Eye Guy," he asked what part of England I called home and I surprised him, explaining that Dallas was home. Our back and forth banter in five different accents revealed that he could mimic them all. I had met my match! When he told me that he taught courses on "Creative Ways to Deal with Fear and Anger," I found that we had at least two things in common: 1) I was developing a series of shows with my newest dummy about fear and anger in children; and 2) my eyes matched a longing in his, seeing there just might be more that we needed to cover. We exchanged business cards and he encouraged me to email and call him, extending a sincere offer to use any of his information in my new program.

When he left I couldn't stop thinking about him and knew that I was about to embark on a journey requiring tremendous courage. With full knowledge that I might get hurt again I took the chance. After all, if I didn't get to know him, I would definitely be hurting myself and miss out on the chance to get to know this amazingly warm, compassionate man with a genuine passion for helping others. I made a choice to begin a journey that has convinced me that his captivating eyes truly were the windows to his soul.

Aunt Cindy and Dr. Keith

Blending two hearts into one might be the most important decision in a lifetime. Each heart shouldn't lose its own identity or shed the characteristics that made it the only one of its kind in all of the world. But for a lifetime of abundance, each heart must find new ways to lift the wants, needs and happiness of the other heart higher than his or her own. On February 12, 2005 the lives of Aunt Cindy and Dr. Keith became one as they were married on the stage of The Country Playhouse in Houston, Texas, before an audience of friends who feasted on the best of Herschel's chocolates.

Happiness and fulfillment can happen as lives start over again. Like magnets, opposites usually attract. Big personality differences make for even bigger surprises as life unfolds. Even on the busiest of days, our eyes meet, reminding us of our beginning. Aunt Cindy never knew she would get coffee and backrubs every morning. And, Dr. Keith never imagined that he would forever live life with "a bunch of dummies."

Dr. Keith A. & Cindy C. Robinson

OUT OF PAIN, ABUNDANCE
Debra J. Berg

Everyone encounters emotional pain in life. But how is it that some people go on to live a life of fulfillment and abundance, while others can never seem to get beyond their painful experiences?

On a fantastic eight-year journey across the United States, I discovered the answer. The journey was comprised of dozens of face-to-face interviews with 150 everyday citizens who had dropped everything in their lives to focus on solving a challenging social problem. The original intent of my interviews was to learn how they had created their successful solutions for targeting crime, poverty, housing shortages, neighborhood decay and at-risk youth. I desperately wanted to know this information because the government had spent billions of dollars trying to solve these very same problems, only to realize rather lackluster results. These citizen-invented ideas were responsible for transforming the lives of millions, and some had even been replicated in dozens of cities across America and around the world. I found the stories to be life transforming, and each interview was another indication that pointed to an exciting new trend I now refer to as "The New Civic America."

When I'm a guest on a radio or television talk show to discuss my journey, the first question is seldom, "How are these people coming up with such great ideas?" Instead, they want to know, "*Why* do they do it?" The public is fascinated by what motivates someone to sacrifice so much for others. That's when I share the one common, but little- known, thread that drives their success. It isn't education, since the levels vary. As they come from a myriad of races, religions and age groups, background isn't the commonality either. Their surroundings don't seem to matter since their ideas were launched under dissimilar circumstances in 30 cities. And while a few could be considered wealthy, most are middle class. What, then, could motivate an average citizen to dismantle his personal life, give up a six-figure income, dissolve a 401K, sell her house or even say good-bye to an NFL pension to launch an altruistic cause? To my surprise, the answer was *emotional pain*. Each one had come through a personally intense emotional experience or had witnessed the suffering and deep emotional pain of others. It was actually out of this experience with pain that they were compelled to act.

Psychologists tell us that pain and pleasure are two of the greatest motivators. Most people will give up a lot to avoid even the smallest painful experience, in order to feel more pleasure. So why would someone be willing to help others overcome *their* pain by enduring even more pain themselves? Take, for example, one woman I met on my journey who sacrificed it all to help at-risk youth. As I learned of her amazing life story, I discovered that an extremely painful experience had built the cornerstone of her relationship with the children.

Tamara Cibis was 9 years old when her wealthy Jewish family fell victim to the Holocaust in Nazi Germany. Her father was killed, along with other family members. She came to the United States as an adult, consumed by years of anger; who could blame her? Eventually, she realized her pain was interfering with her relationships. It was only when her heart softened in response to the plight of minority youth who were suffering a similar type of discrimination that her anger was mitigated. She'd observed that the only way these youth knew how to respond to bigotry and racism was to lash out in retaliation toward others. Most of them came from broken and drug-infested homes as well. Missing from their lives was unconditional love and someone to point them away from bad habits and self-destruction. That's when Tamara decided to give up a six-figure income to live in a run-down house on the rough side of a Midwestern town just to build a relationship with the African American children. Her goal was to help them learn new ways of dealing with discrimination.

The long-haired, blond German woman was certainly conspicuous and intimidating to some in the black neighborhood. The difference was enough to bring about threats to her life, as well as property damage and even physical abuse. But Tamara was more concerned with building a relationship with the kids and stood fast to her plan. Months went by before the kids finally began to feel comfortable dropping by her front porch to chat, but little by little they came to trust Tamara. They could identify with her story and she taught them better ways to respond, despite their circumstances. She even involved the neighborhood grand-mothers as role models who offered the children a safe haven and snacks after school. Tamara's plan, which was funded out of donations, volunteers and a meager budget, evolved into the initiatives of Matthew House and the Grandparent Home Missions Program.

Today, 20 years later, Tamara has successfully rescued more than 1,000 boys and girls from a future of welfare and imprisonment. It's difficult to measure her influence on future generations; when counting dollars and cents, we know the state taxpayers will save at least $3 billion in future incarceration and welfare costs. But there's yet another bonus: Tamara's programs, recently adopted by Catholic Charities, are being replicated by more cities and neighborhoods all across America! Like a phoenix rising out of the ashes of pain, Tamara's decision to sublimate her anger to help children lead productive lives has since translated into untold abundance for thousands of youth and their families.

Not everyone who encounters pain will decide to sacrifice so much of him or herself to help others, but each amazing interview I held with citizens like Tamara revealed the same message: Intense emotional pain produces vast quantities of un-harnessed energy. That energy can either be transformed into passion for good, or internalized to the point that it consumes the individual. It's up to us to choose.

My mother used to refer to it as "turning lemons into lemonade." Others might call it "making the best of a bad situation." The power of one person to make a difference is often as close as our own pain turned inside out. Do you recall the last time you felt like a victim? The next time you do and are inclined to succumb to feelings of powerlessness and insignificance, try to remember Tamara's example. Like her, if you view your "pain energy" as a gift and decide to re-invest the golden lessons that you've learned in the lives of others, you'll be on the doorstep to a new abundant life. And who knows? Your newly transformed energy might even change the world!

 Debra J. Berg

EMBRACE SILENCE
Dr. Wayne Dyer

You live in a noisy world, constantly bombarded with loud music, sirens, construction equipment, jet airplanes, rumbling trucks, leaf blowers, lawn mowers and tree cutters. These manmade, unnatural sounds invade your senses and keep silence at bay.

In fact, you've been raised in a culture that not only eschews silence, but is terrified of it. The car radio must always be on, and any pause in conversation is a moment of embarrassment that most people quickly fill with chatter. For many, being alone in silence is pure torture.

The famous scientist Blaise Pascal observed, "All man's miseries derive from not being able to sit quietly in a room alone."

With practice, you can become aware that there's a momentary silence in the space between your thoughts. In this silent space, you'll find the peace that you crave in your daily life. You'll never know that peace if you don't have any spaces between your thoughts.

The average person is said to have 60,000 separate thoughts a day. With so many thoughts, there are almost no gaps. If you could reduce that number by half, you would open up an entire world of possibilities for yourself. For it is when you merge into the silence, and become one with it, that you reconnect to your source and know the peacefulness that some call "God." It is stated beautifully in Psalms of the Old Testament: "Be still and know that I am God." The key words are "still" and "know."

"Still" actually means "silence." Mother Teresa described silence and its relationship to God by saying, "God is the friend of silence. See how nature (trees, grass) grows in silence. We need silence to be able to touch souls." This includes your soul.

It's really the space between the notes that make the music you enjoy so much. Without the spaces, all you would have is one continuous, noisy note. Everything that's created comes out of silence. Your thoughts emerge from the nothingness of silence. Your words come out of this void. Your very essence emerged from emptiness.

All creativity requires some stillness. Your sense of inner peace depends on spending some of your life energy in silence to recharge your batteries, removing tension and anxiety, thus reacquainting you with the joy of knowing God and feeling closer to all of humanity. Silence reduces fatigue and allows you to experience your own creative juices.

The second word in the Old Testament observation, "know," refers to making your personal and conscious contact with God. To know God is to banish doubt and become independent of others' definitions and descriptions of God. Instead, you have your own personal knowing. And, as Melville reminded us so poignantly, "God's one and only voice is silence."

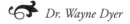 *Dr. Wayne Dyer*

LITTLE WISDOM
Mary Gates

Amaya felt the squish of tacky mud between her soft, white fingers. She noticed the firm grains of sand that were held in place with the dark paste of clay and wondered if real houses were ever built from earth, the way her pretend houses were.

Amaya loved the mud—it could easily be sculpted into anything she dreamed. Some days, the mud spoke to her and told her what it wanted to be—a family of frogs, a flower garden, a casserole, a fully-furnished apartment.

One of her favorite activities was carving a long trough of mud into a riverbank and lining it with the most beautiful stones she could find. On truly abundant days, her mother gave her permission to turn on the garden hose for awhile and build a real stream that danced down the entire hillside next to her house!

Amaya was often inspired to create neighborhood villages for her friends, the "Little People," who lived in her mind and told outrageous stories about fairies, werewolves, goddesses and pixies. Amaya wasn't even sure she knew what a pixie was, but the "Little People" always filled her in when she had questions for them. They never volunteered information, but they always answered her questions once she could formulate them.

One of Amaya's most steadfast friends in the mud was Kate—a steady, timeless tree who always gave her shade and wisdom. Amaya often talked with Kate about things she couldn't share with her parents. Kate warned her to never be alone with the older boy who lived down the street, and she gave her words for the second-grade bully: "That's a dumb way to act and I'm not going to be any part of it!"

Other friends among the "Little People" included Moira and grand-motherly Anna. Moira was a round, clever woman with a sharp tongue and shiny, coffee-colored skin that sparkled when she smiled. Moira didn't waste any words on nonsense, and Amaya always knew it was the absolute truth when Moira spoke.

The "Little People" friends drifted in and out through the weeks and years of Amaya's childhood. When she saw red and black plaid, it usually meant that long-legged, stunning Ingrid was close. Ingrid always made Amaya feel like she could stand up just a little taller. A sour smell usually triggered an appearance from Ronny, who reminded Amaya to show kindness to everyone, even if they smelled bad or were otherwise unpleasant.

Amaya knew that her parents were unhappy. She could see that bills were arriving faster than customers, and Amaya wondered how much longer her parents would be able to keep their restaurant open. She heard her father's tense words long after the lights were out, and she knew why her mother's pillow was often wet and smeared with mascara in the afternoons when Amaya came home from school.

Amaya could feel the loneliness of her parents' marriage, yet she didn't know how to reach into the darkness with comfort or companionship. She decided that her parents probably had no "Little People" to talk with about their problems. *"They would have good advice and help for all their problems, if only they knew the 'Little People,'"* she thought.

Amaya began to imagine what it would be like for her parents to get to know the "Little People." One day, she asked Kate the Tree how they could be introduced to each other. Kate told Amaya that she should invite Aunt Nancy over for a visit.

"Have you ever met your Divine Team?" asked Aunt Nancy a few days later.

"I don't know," Amaya's mother replied. "What do you mean by 'Divine Team'?"

"It's a group of spirit creatures who can help you along in your journey of life," explained Aunt Nancy. She told all about having regular meetings with her own Divine Team, and how they answered questions for her and showed her where to find important tools, people and information.

Amaya's ears prickled and her heart began to flutter. She knew this was exactly what her parents needed!

Amaya's mother squirmed and could only say, "Hmm…tell me more."

"Would you like to meet them?" Aunt Nancy asked.

"Who?" puzzled Amaya's mother.

"Your Divine Team."

"My 'Divine Team'? What makes you think I have a Divine Team?"

Amaya thought about God and how only recently she had come to understand that God was actually living inside of her—not only living there, but also breathing into her, filling her with love and actually *being* her—along with everything else, too. She didn't know how to classify this strange idea of a "Divine Team" and had never before considered the possibility that there could be multiple divine creatures to assist and support her.

"Close your eyes," Aunt Nancy instructed. "Good. Let yourself be filled with love, light, peace…and the deepest gratitude you ever knew. Allow the breath of life to fill your entire being, all the way from the top of your head to the tips of your fingertips and toes." Amaya gazed in awe as her mother followed Aunt Nancy's instructions.

Amaya soon found herself evaporating into relaxed consciousness with
Aunt Nancy and her mother. She welcomed the familiar warm buzz that
melted her skin and made her eyebrows tickle.

After a few minutes, Nancy asked "Do you see a door?" as one strangely
made itself known to Amaya. It was a beautiful, old wooden door—
faded mocha, heavily carved with soft, geometric forms. It reminded her
of something she might have seen in a picture of an aging Medieval
church building in one of her father's old European travel guidebooks.
Her mind began to drift to her father's stories of the lovely people of
South Central Europe and how they had befriended him when he was
wandering through the Pohorje Hills of Slovenia long before Amaya was
born.

Aunt Nancy's voice brought her back to the door. "OK, when you are
ready, open the door. Go in and meet your Divine Team—they've been
waiting for you."

"Could it really be that easy?" Amaya wondered, as she noticed that her
hand was reaching for the lever of the door. It slowly crept open, and
Amaya looked inside with awe. Her dear friends, the "Little People,"
were waiting for her!

Amaya began to tremble. Her limbs melted into the earth as her spirit
floated up and away, drifting gently into another dimension. The feeling
was familiar, and Amaya recognized it as the sensation of surrendering
to anesthesia before surgery when she had her tonsils removed a few
months ago.

Suddenly, Amaya felt a new steadiness at her side, and she turned to see
her mother glowing beside her as they swiftly guided each other into the
room. They were greeted by Anna and her long, silken, silver hair.
Anna's soft bosom and the scent of sweet sandalwood embraced Amaya
as she and her mother were both enveloped in love.

They were all there—old, familiar friends among the comforting aroma of damp earth. Moira, Kate, Ingrid (still wearing plaid!) and even Paul; the wispy fluff of bright, changing colors that seemed to live happily without any tangible body at all. Sparks of stars and swirls of lights surrounded them—each one another spirit creature waiting to be introduced.

Amaya knew help had arrived!

 *Mary Gates*

FINDING YOUR FITNESS PURPOSE
Brian J. Johnston

Are you living the life, enjoying the health and experiencing the level of abundance you once wished for? If you respond with "yes," I offer genuine congratulations. If not, is there a deep longing or sense that you could do, be and, therefore, have more? It is like an incessant *drip...drip...drip...*reminding us the leaky faucet needs repair.

No matter the frantic pace at which you fly through each day, no matter how much you fill your schedule, no matter where you go, what you do, what you buy or who you pretend to be, it's *always* there, isn't it? That pesky little mental monster you continue to wrestle with—"***be more, do more, have more!***" *drip...drip...drip...*

The good news is there's victory waiting in the wings! For, just as a loving parent or skilled teacher is unwilling to settle for less than what a child or student is truly capable of, God desires and expects the same from us. And, as a child of God—created by Him, for Him—the *drip...drip...drip...*of the Holy Spirit encourages each of us to actively seek, discover and successfully live out the ultimate purpose for which we were designed.

Biblical Abundance Basics
Throughout the Bible, God provides a detailed blueprint for living an abundant and meaningful life. Along with it comes the ability, or free will, to make our own decisions about what we will think, say or do at any given moment. We also find the earliest recorded example of what's considered to be good business sense today.

With infinite wisdom and love, God provides a succinct, yet powerful, "disclaimer" for us to consider prior to transacting any thought, word or deed: *"A man reaps what he sows."* (Gal. 6:7, NIV)

This simple message instructs, encourages and forewarns us that life is a series of choices, generally governed by laws of cause and effect. Entrusted with the freedom of personal choice, it's therefore wise to remember to control what we think, say and do. For this determines in what direction we will ultimately travel. The lesson: Poor choices usually result in unpleasant consequences.

With regard to the care, development and maintenance of our bodies, one of the best choices to make would be to ignore what the world—TV, magazines, movie stars, etc.—feverishly peddles as "the way." The constant bombardment and allure of instant gratification and hyped-up marketing only fuels the fire of frustration for those who buy into such empty, profit-driven madness.

Slick promotional campaigns promise to deliver instant happiness and fulfill every desire for those who can attain the ultra-cool, highly-exclusive privilege of "*Right* Club" status. Membership is generally automatic if you make or have the *right* amount of money, wear the *right* clothes, have the *right* body, drive the *right* car, live in the *right* home in the *right* neighborhood, send your kids to the *right* school, eat at the *right* places or meet the *right* people by hanging out at the *right* hotspot.

But what if you don't currently have membership privileges? No problem. All you need to do is undergo the right vanity-based procedure (or series of them) to finally have the *right* body, and you can join the *right* gym, eat the *right* food, take the *right* pills, move into the *right* neighborhood, mingle with the *right* people.... Then your life instantly becomes enjoyable because you make or have the *right* amount of money, have the *right* body so you can wear the *right* clothes, drive the *right* car, blah, blah, blah.... Right?

Drip...drip...drip...

Attempting to fill the void with material things, a smaller dress size, six-pack abs, greater status or whatever else the world can get you to buy into doesn't lead to an abundant life, everlasting health or fulfill the ultimate purpose for which you so desperately seek to experience. Has it ever *really* done so before?

Drip…drip…drip…

Many people are familiar with the phrase *"fearfully and wonderfully made"* (Psalm 139:14), but rarely do they delve deeper into what that actually means or how to genuinely "love the skin you're in" without jumping aboard the current fad-wagon. The problem is compounded by the futile attempts—hoping, wishing, yearning—to fill the deep, longing, intangible needs of the heart and soul (love, peace, joy, hope) with shallow, fleeting, material things (money, clothes, cars, sex, plastic surgery…) that are shamelessly glamorized by today's culture.

The reality is that the sooner we forego the emptiness of instant "get-ification" and begin the process of building a more fulfilling, deeply satisfying and eternally significant existence, the better! God provides specific instructions on how to develop and maintain an abundant, awe-inspiring level of health and happiness. You just have to know where to look.

"Whatever is true, whatever is noble, whatever is right, whatever is pure, whatever is lovely, whatever is admirable—if anything is excellent or praiseworthy—think about such things." (Phil. 4:8)

Do you truly desire an abundant life, to improve yourself in some way, or to experience a greater sense of peace, joy and fulfillment? Would you like to transcend your current circumstances, with the ability to see the "big picture" from an aerial perspective that comes from God? The Old Testament verse says, *"Remove far from me vanity and lies: give me neither poverty nor riches; feed me with food convenient for me."* (Prov. 30:8)

Begin by seeking guidance from the One who created it all in the first place. Everything you need to get started can be easily acquired:

- Instruction manual (the Bible)
- Accountability partner (family, friend, or small group)
- 24/7 Call Center (prayer)

By utilizing these resources on a regular basis, you'll soon discover an abundant supply of health, fitness, nutrition, beauty and happiness "secrets" according to God. *"Don't worry about anything; instead, pray about everything; tell God your needs and don't forget to thank Him for His answers. If you do this you will experience God's peace, which is far more wonderful than the human mind can understand."* (Phil. 4:6-7)

It is my personal mission and business vision to use this information to educate, encourage and equip you to ultimately influence others. As you read this, may your thoughts, words and deeds be directed by God and your ultimate purpose be made clear.

I pray others may benefit from you relationally, because out of you flows a renewed sense of joy, peace and fulfillment. This becomes a powerful personal testimony of how incredibly patient, merciful and loving God can be once we are willing to seek and serve Him above all things.

 *Brian J. Johnston*

LIVING A BLESSED LIFE
David Mason

I was the first in my family to attend University. I began my career as a Research Biologist at an Agriculture Canada research farm. Although I loved the work I was doing, I became increasingly frustrated with the direction of my career and realized for the first time what work-related stress was.

I decided it was time to explore my entrepreneurial urges. I had no business experience, as neither of my parents had been in business, but I had always wanted to start my own business and I thought I had come up with a great idea for a service: home inspections. It wasn't until I did a market survey that I realized that this was already an extremely well-developed industry. I contacted the leading home inspection franchise for more information, and they courted me for about 10 months. I finally decided to take a huge leap of faith: I gave up the security of a steady paycheck and bought a license to service northern Nova Scotia and southern New Brunswick. If you are familiar with this part of Atlantic Canada, you know this is a fairly large geographic area with a relatively low population density.

The early years were tough, as the industry was relatively unknown in my area at the time. In the beginning, all I concentrated on was name recognition. When someone asked what a home inspection was and who did them, I wanted my name to slip out of the mouth of the person they were asking before they even realized they had said it. I focused on the marketing and my business grew.

I grew increasingly busy until, one day, I had an epiphany. I realized I had gotten into business for myself in order to have a better quality of life, but I had given up my life for the business. It had gotten to the point that I was tired of my work and it had become my life. I just wanted to start over but I felt stuck. The feeling of being trapped was terrible; I dreaded each day. At that point, I decided it wasn't working for me, and if I was going to continue, my family and I had to come first. This will sound clichéd, but I started working smarter—not harder—and I was able to work *on* the business, as well as *in* the business. My business began to grow even more and I had a life again.

This led to another epiphany. I realized that home inspection was not my calling. As much as I enjoyed it and felt proficient at it, I wanted to play a bigger game. After a lot of soul searching and introspection, I guess you could say I "woke up." I came up with a mission for my life and my business, and I still use it to this day. My mission is this: *To help people become more successful so that I can help those who cannot help themselves to live a better quality of life.*

I now realized I was going to need to invest in an ongoing education. I was trained in professional speaking. I became a certified coach, a certified trainer and a board certified hypnotherapist. I started traveling North America to meet with the gurus and to attend seminars, workshops and training. I had a voracious appetite for learning and I consumed an enormous amount of information. I continue to do so to this day.

I started to develop my new business while still operating my home inspection business full-time. I guess this would be a good time to define "full-time." You see, I stopped working evenings and weekends because that, to me, is family time. I took Wednesday as my personal and professional development day—I worked only four days a week. That may not sound impressive, but in the home inspection industry, that is an anomaly. Here I am making a comfortable six-figure income while working only four days a week.

I decided that in order to build momentum for my new business, I would write a book. With no previous book writing or publishing experience, I wrote *Marketing Your Small Business For Big Profits*. I was able to get endorsements from some giants in the marketing industry, self-published the book, got it listed on Amazon.com (a daunting task) and arranged a launch. As a result of hard work and some good fortune, my book became a best-seller on Amazon.com, which was more than I could have hoped for.

But I couldn't take my new business any farther while still running a full-time home inspection business. It had become the shackle that kept me from soaring with my new business. So I decided to sell my home inspection business. Now, that was easier said than done because it was almost 100 percent referral based; I couldn't risk advertising the business for sale for fear of losing the referrals. It became a catch 22. Although I don't have time to tell that story here, I can say my prayers were answered by what can only be explained as a miracle, and, happily, I sold the business.

I now operate Mason Performance Development Inc.—a speaking, training and coaching company—full-time. My success with my book on Amazon attracted the interest of a New York publisher. I have signed with the publisher and my book has been re-released; it has become an international best-seller, and is now available as a hardcover and paperback from all major online and offline bookstores. As a performance development coach and trainer, I now help small business owners and entrepreneurs overcome obstacles and sticking points. By turning adversity into opportunity, increasing confidence and focus, and by taking purposeful action, my clients make more money in less time, and thereby take their business and their lives to the next level.

I am now living on purpose and have more zest for life. I am taking better care of my body and I have even more time for my family. I have incorporated my mission from the grass roots of my business. A portion of the proceeds from every copy of my book sold goes to Habitat for Humanity. Therefore, I am helping people who otherwise would not get that chance to realize their dream of home ownership. It feels good to know I am making a difference.

If an unknown person from a small town in Nova Scotia can go from being stuck to becoming a best-selling author, coaching others to their success and living a blessed life of abundance, then there is no reason you can't start living the life YOU love.

Here's to YOUR success!

 David Mason

SEE WHAT YOU WANT
Bill Harris

Until about age 40, I was definitely not living the life I loved. I was chronically angry, often depressed, and had one abysmal relationship after another. I had no real career and no idea how to create one. The direction of my life was down or, at best, sideways.

This was all a blessing in disguise though, because it created an intense motivation to learn what happy, peaceful and successful people did that I wasn't doing.

Today, I'm married to a wonderful woman who really loves me. I make ten times what I used to fantasize about. Plus, I have a challenging career doing something I love.

My anger problem is gone, and I haven't been depressed for even a minute in nearly 15 years.

Now, at age 54, I truly am living the life I love. This transformation happened when I discovered a few key principles that created tremendous positive change for me. They will work for you, too.

What are these secrets?

First, happy people acknowledge that they are creating their reality internally and externally. They see circumstances as an influence, but know that what they do inside creates how they feel and behave and what people and situations they draw to themselves.

For most people, processing external circumstances happens unconsciously. This makes it seem as if circumstances cause your feelings, behavior, and what you attract into your life. When this happens, it seems as if you are the effect of external causes over which you have no control.

Happy people, however, even if they can't see how, know they're creating whatever is happening. They take responsibility.

Another characteristic of happy people is that their actions are the result of the possibilities they see. Where the unhappy person sees a challenge as impossible, the happy person sees what is possible. And, by focusing on what is possible, happy people make those possibilities come true.

A third characteristic of happy, successful people: They focus their minds on what they want and keep their mind off of what they do not want.

Take prosperity, for instance. You could focus on not being poor, or you could focus on being rich. That is, you could make a mental picture of poverty, wanting to avoid it, or you could create a picture of being wealthy, wanting to move toward it.

In both cases, the intention is the same, but your brain doesn't care about your intentions. It just sees the literal content of the picture. When you focus on riches, it thinks you want riches and motivates you to see opportunities, find resources and take action to be rich.

When you focus on not being poor, it sees a picture of being poor and motivates you to see opportunities, find resources and take action…to be poor.

Most people focus on what they want to avoid without realizing the consequences. When they get what they didn't want, they assume they didn't focus hard enough and redouble their efforts. This creates even more of what they don't want, which creates more frustration.

The other penalty for focusing on what you don't want is that you feel bad. In fact, all bad feelings and negative outcomes are the result of focusing on what you do not want. Instead of unconsciously and automatically focusing on what you don't want, consciously and intentionally focus on what you do want. When you do this, you instantly begin to create it, and you instantly feel good.

The final characteristic: Happy people are consciously aware. As a result, their brains are less likely to run on automatic, creating internal states and external outcomes they did not intend and do not want.

First, become more consciously aware through meditation. Though traditional meditation is very beneficial, at Centerpointe Research Institute we use an audio technology called Holosync to create deep, meditative states, literally at the push of a button. This greatly accelerates the meditation process and allows you to create increased conscious awareness very quickly.

Second, investigate your own beliefs, values, ways of filtering information, strategies for decision making, motivations and other internal processes. Centerpointe's Life Principles Integration Process is a structured way of investigating and changing these internal processes, allowing you to take charge of how you create your internal and external results.

There is a price to pay to live the life you love. But paying it is a joyful enterprise that will benefit you for the rest of your life. You create your reality, so learn to focus your mind on what you want, and increase your conscious awareness through meditation and self-inquiry.

The life you love is waiting for you!

 *Bill Harris*

An Attitude of Abundance, Always
Ben Sutter

Is it possible to have too much abundance? Is there a way to increase the abundance in our lives? Those of us who live in the United States are immediately blessed with freedom of choice and a standard of living that is amazing. Our attitude about living abundantly is even more important than the physical reality of where we live. By aligning ourselves with positive expectations and vibrations, we can attract all the abundance that we desire into our lives. We can choose whether or not we will live in and attract abundance.

Once, when I was farming, a combine caught on fire. These huge machines are vital to farming and cost as much as many family homes do. Our fire extinguishers didn't even touch the rapidly spreading flames as the fire consumed the machine. The bright flames in the night sky drew neighbors to the action. One of them commented that I didn't seem upset by the fire. I replied that since no one was hurt and because I had a second combine in the field, I was just going to enjoy the flames in the clear night sky and replace the combine later. A piece of steel can always be replaced.

I finished that harvest with only one combine, and before the next harvest I replaced the burned machine with one of the same model that was just as good as the one I'd lost. Plus, I bought my neighbor's harvesting head so that I would have a second one of the preferred type. By keeping an attitude of abundance, I was able to improve my situation.

Victor Frankel wrote of his experience in a Nazi concentration camp. He stated that the one thing that can't be taken away from us is the power to form our own thoughts. No matter what situation we find ourselves in, it can be a positive experience if we keep our thoughts on things of beauty and creating mental images of our ideal life. If we keep our focus and expectations on abundance, the Law of Attraction will reward us with more of it.

My challenges have included left side paralysis, blindness in my left eye, and stuttering. Because I know that my purpose is to share my abundance with others, I have chosen not to be limited by adversity and to keep my focus on the abundance that I experience every day. For this reason, I pursued becoming a Passion Test facilitator to help other people recognize and achieve their ideal lives. As Chris and Janet Attwood, the authors of the book The Passion Test, taught me: following my passion is the real difference in activating the Law of Attraction. Abundance flows toward people who are passionate about what they are doing.

The physical issues that I first perceived to be limitations turned out to be the key building blocks needed in my development. Things that first appear to be terrible events give us the richness of experience and the depth to fully appreciate what we have and all the incremental gains in abundance that we experience every day. We are the sum of how we react to what life has handed us as we hone our abundant attitude.

Joyful living can be achieved at whatever level of abundance you are currently experiencing, and greater abundance provides a platform to enhance your comfort, which, in turn, will enhance your creativity. This creativity will allow you to better serve others and to circulate the abundance back into the world.

Associating with positive people is one of my passions, and it can be an integral part of preventing negative thoughts from gaining a foothold. We all have our moments of doubt or negativity, and if we can actively replace these thoughts with positive images, our progress will continue.

One part of the Law of Attraction states that the supply of abundance is unlimited; therefore, we can never take more than our share. The universe wants us to have everything we desire. We need to create an image in our minds of the good things that we would like to have or experience in our lives, keep it in our consciousness with frequent reminders and then allow the universe to provide those things.

Vision boards and goal or passion lists are great tools to reinforce the things we want to attract into our lives by bringing them into our conscious and subconscious mind. A picture of your dream house gives your mind the input it needs, as does a clearly defined list of your goals or passions.

By clearly knowing what form you want your abundance to take, you can make choices to encourage the manifestation. Clarity is a very empowering tool, as the universe doesn't like ambiguity when we make our requests for abundance. Sometimes the universe knows better than we do what we really want or need, so it can be good to say, "I want that, or something better."

With abundance out there looking for us, we need to accept it and allow it to happen by maintaining a constant state of gratitude. The more practice we have at giving heartfelt thanks for our many blessings every day, the more the universe will recognize us as a worthy conduit of abundance, and the longer our list of everyday things to be grateful for will become.

We need to fully recognize and love the abundance that we have right now and be ready for the waves of abundance that will surely follow. I am grateful for a loving God, health, family, wealth, an active mind, the opportunity to study and share personal growth ideas and the ability to speak and write about my passions in life. When I began being thankful about these things, I had a lot less to be thankful for than I do now, and I know this is just the beginning.

Positive thoughts and vibrations will stimulate the delivery of the abundance we crave and deserve if we follow these ideas. If negative thoughts are trying to influence you, use a clearing technique such as saying, "Cancel." Positive thoughts are more powerful than negative thoughts, and you need to create room for them by purging the negative thoughts. Affirmations, meditation and prayer are all good methods of calming the mind, getting into in a state of gratitude, and connecting with the images of what will make your life ideal.

Claim the abundance that you deserve, because the universe has it waiting for you if you are clear about what you want. Waiting to claim your abundance isn't an option. NOW is your time!

Ben Sutter

A REMARKABLE STRANGER WHO TRANSFORMED MY LIFE
Ruth Kuttler

For most of my first 45 years of life, I didn't really know who I was or what I was here to do. I was stuck in a place called "mediocrity"—I was unhappy and unfulfilled. I believed that "settling" was my lot in life and that I just had to accept it.

I grew up in a family in which nothing I did was ever quite good enough. My mother's dream was to become a nurse, and when it came time for me to decide on a career, I became the nurse she had always wanted to be. The first day I set foot in a hospital, I wanted to run the other way. But my family and fiancé convinced me that nursing was a great profession for a woman. Besides that, I grew up believing the fairytale that a woman's career didn't matter—it was just something to fall back on in case she had to work. Before I knew it, I was married and my husband and I were struggling to make ends meet, even with both of us working full-time. Over the next several years, our salaries doubled and tripled. With each increase in pay, however, we found more and more ways to spend the extra money—we both wanted a nice home, clothes, cars and a little traveling here and there. It didn't take long before I was dependent on every penny of my nurse's salary.

Every day I came home from work drained—physically and emotionally exhausted. I kept thinking that a different job would make me happy. I went from one position to another, desperate to find a sense of personal satisfaction and fulfillment. When that didn't work, I went back to school, initially for a master's degree and later for a post-master's certification as a family nurse practitioner—the ultimate nursing position. Instead of contentment, I felt even more stressed and miserable, like a powerless animal trapped in a cage.

Finally, an opportunity presented itself in the spring of 1998. Although it didn't feel like an opportunity at the time, the lay-off from my job turned out to be a blessing in disguise. I went through the motions of looking for work and became deeply depressed. I wished I had other choices but didn't believe there were any other options for me—I had no other skills or abilities that would land me a decent paying job and replace my nurse practitioner's salary.

During this time, I asked God why I was here and what I should do with my life. Sometimes God responds in strange and mysterious ways. The answer to my prayers came on a Sunday when I was going through the newspaper looking for work. While searching through the employment section, I came across an advertisement for a poetry contest. I was not a poet and didn't even like most poetry, but for some reason, I kept going back to that contest page and thinking to myself, "Maybe if I write about what I am feeling, I'll figure out what I should be doing with the rest of my life." Although I had always been a very good writer, I had never given myself an opportunity to write creatively. I sat down to write a poem, which I called "Going Not Where I Know." Before I knew it, I couldn't stop writing—words and messages set to rhythmical patterns from deep inside my soul were pouring out onto paper. I didn't put my pen down for almost three weeks. There were days that I wrote for 12 to 14 hours—didn't get dressed, do dishes, do laundry or even make meals. There I sat, at my kitchen table, in my nightgown, writing one poem after another.

Not only did my poetry connect me with a gift and passion that I didn't know I had, it led to a transformational effect on my life. Through my poetry, I was compelled to listen to my heart. There, I discovered my higher self—a pipeline to God and keys to a happy and prosperous life. I no longer saw limits—only abundant possibilities and opportunities. I came to understand how my thoughts had created my experiences, both good and bad. Just like other unhappy people, I had created my own story, limiting my life by erroneous beliefs that I held to be true about myself.

For the first time in my life, I felt empowered to do whatever it took to design the life I really wanted. I vowed to let go of self-limiting beliefs and fears and distanced myself from unsupportive people. I immersed myself in self-help books and attended every personal development seminar I could find. Little by little, I began to believe in myself and in possibilities for creating the life I really wanted—a life abundant in happiness and fulfillment. I committed to a plan and to do whatever it took to bring that plan to fruition. As my heart and passion became my guide, I discovered who I was and what I was here to do. Within myself, I found an amazing stranger—a strong, courageous woman who transformed my life.

It is now 10 years later. I wake up every day energized, happy, fulfilled and eager to start my day. Not only do I own my own web development and marketing company, I am an award-winning inspirational speaker, award-winning poet, author and graphic artist. What I've learned is that there is nothing extraordinary about me that allowed me to transition from a miserable existence to living my dream. We all have the ability to create a happy, fulfilling life—it is all about the messages that we tell ourselves and the choices that we make.

There is nothing that exhilarates me more than to share my story and reach out and inspire someone to achieve his or her happiest life. I now spend much of my time sharing the wisdom I acquired with others—people who want to live a happy and prosperous life; people who want to join me, living in abundance.

 *Ruth Kuttler*

REVEALING YOUR HEART-SONG
Linda Hannah Young

Have you ever stood on a beach and watched the sun set into the ocean, or watched a child lovingly put arms around the neck of a loved one? Have you ever seen the look in your dog's eye when you've walked into a room and seen the excitement that is generated because he or she is pleased to see you? All of these moments are tiny gateways to your "Heart-Song." They are warm and tender, and they find their way into your innermost being.

What would life be like if, instead of occasionally being surprised when we feel it resonating inside of us, we lived by our Heart-Songs all of the time?

Your Heart-Song is the music inside of you—the true vibration of who you really are. It is your essence, made in the image of God. Some refer to it as your "Being," "Sub-Conscious" or "Inner Light." The name doesn't matter as much as the meaning, but it is this that I am passionate about. It is a song that must be "sung" in order for the real you to be revealed, and in so doing, others are able to be inspired by it!

So what stops your Heart-Song from being able to sing out all of the time? Unfortunately, for some it is so heavily buried underneath critical voices, self-condemnation and ego that it is all but suffocated. It is so buried under business, schedules and expectations that its melodic resonance is muted to the detriment of yourself and the world.

From the beginning of our lives we have countless influences upon us. These include our parents, caretakers, siblings, teachers, culture, gender and countless others. Some of these influences will nurture and nourish our Heart-Song, while others will flatten and steamroll it. Let me give you examples from my own life. As a child, I fancied myself as a bit of an artist. I loved to paint and draw, and because my grandfather painted, I was sure that I had inherited the skill from him. As I stood at my easel at no more than 10 years of age, I caught the eye of my art teacher who was passing by me. He looked at my painting and I thought, "Here is my chance." So I said to him, "My Grandfather is an artist!" He gave me a strange look and said, "Don't mix the colors in the pallet; someone else may need to use it." My Heart-Song, which I had sung to him with great vulnerability, was overwhelmed by a deafening silence of no recognition that day. I did not allow the artistic notes of my Heart-Song to be heard by others for many years following that event.

On the positive side, after doing a few individual units during theological college, I was approached by a lecturer and asked to consider ministry. When I reflected on the things he had said to me, I realized that the faculty had been watching me and had actually heard my Heart-Song without my knowledge! The invitation from them began a formation process, and through that process my Heart-Song was heard and even applauded at times. How wonderful!

Like most people, i have had times of rejection and times of acceptance in my life. Part of my deepest maturing has been when I have recognized the times when my Heart-Song has not been heard, noticed or appreciated. These were the times when deeply implicit growth within me later became evident.

My younger brother is over six feet tall and has an amazing bass baritone voice. One of the things he loves to do is to allow his family and friends to put their heads against his chest and listen to the resonation of his deepest note. It is such an amazing sound! It is not his greatest volume, but the sound is ostensibly internal. It is so incredibly deep that it sends shivers down my spine. This is similar your internal Heart-Song, which resonates deep within, but usually has no audience. Like the Heart-Song, it is deep and mysterious, penetrating the most inner spaces of the soul.

Sometimes the Heart-Song has been confined for so long that much emotion precedes its re-entrance to the outside world. When something so precious has been suppressed for a great amount of time, a dirge—a dark cry of hurt and pain—may be the first sound to become exposed. But with enough time, however, one's true Heart-Song may slowly begin to re-emerge. When it does emerge and is held with precious respect and truly listened to for all its melodies, harmonies and nuances, this is when the magic begins!

There are so many amazing people who have been able to allow their Heart-Song to sing, despite horribly cruel conditions and circumstances. Some of these include Nelson Mandela, whose Heart-Song was not destroyed by prolonged imprisonment and who is able to sing a tune for so many of us to follow, and Mother Teresa, who chose poverty in order to help the people whom others had rejected to begin to reveal their own Heart-Song. Another example is Steve Irwin, who was able to "translate" the Heart-Song of animals to us so that our ears could begin to hear their true songs. The list goes on and on and does not only include famous people. We all know people in our own lives whose Heart-Song is clear, strong and easily heard!

It is my own life journey and the experiences I have gained through Spiritual Direction that have inspired me to write my new book, *Revealing Your Heart-Song.* It is my passion to help people to uncover their own Heart-Songs and not to restrict them any longer! What the world needs is authentic inhabitants who are willing to allow their Heart-Songs to join with the Heart-Songs of others in order for the greatest musical symphony of all time to be created. What would this look like? In my mind, it would mean accepting others for their own Heart-Song and not trying to impose the tune of others upon them. It means that each and every person, animal, mountain and plain has its own individual and valid Heart-Song that needs to be heard and appreciated for what it is. It's about all of us playing our Heart-Songs together to make a song like no other that has been ever heard before! Can you imagine it? The wonderful thing is that everyone's unique part is needed to make it whole and complete!

What would it take for your Heart-Song to be free to sing its beautiful, unique melody to the world? You must identify those things that are inhibiting your Heart-Song from being fully expressed and find a space that begins to reveal the real you, the essence of you, your Heart-Song, to the world. The world will be a better place as each one of us, individually, works to open our own vocal chords and project to the world our unique Heart-Song. A symphony awaits!

Linda Hannah Young

BEING TRUE
Jane MacAllister Dukes

My middle name is truth. My credo is "speak true and be true—align yourself with your essence and you cannot go wrong." Life is a living, wondrous, co-creative adventure. I can feel it pulsing through my veins even as I write!

I always knew I had a greater purpose. I studied, read, and followed my heart, if not always entirely trusting my instincts. Now I know that I knew more than I realized at the time. I was passionate, loving and generous, but I found it difficult to receive. I have since learned differently.

The big tragedies in my life included: my pony dying when I was 14, my father dying when I was 26, dealing with my sister's suicide when I was 37, and, at 42, miscarrying a baby boy at four months gestation. In between, there were smaller, less significant tragedies, as well as joys, wonders and seriously sensational moments. I was moved by so much, and I knew that I was deeply loved, even if I could not explain why; though, sometimes, I felt very alone—a kind of soul loneliness, seemingly impossible to fill.

Each one of the awful, excruciatingly painful tragedies seared and opened me more, and each one of them bestowed great gifts upon me. Each of the joys and wonders in between expanded my world as well. Life was filled with magic; I saw and felt God everywhere. I could have done without the terrible pain, grief and loss, but I always knew there was a bigger picture, even if I couldn't see it at the time. Slowly but surely, I was opening to receive.

Now, I no longer feel alone. I love myself, this world, and everything in it. I see more positive things than negative. I have moved from life happening to me to being life walking! I am a "lightworker." I am also an artist, creator, mother, lover, coach, cook, cleaner, chairwoman, company director, poet, singer, producer, coordinator, gardener, writer and probably a few other things as well.

The most important thing in my life is my family. My children, 13 and 7, are the delight of my life. It is an honor and a privilege to co-create my daily life with them and my extremely intelligent, well-disguised husband. I am lucky enough to have wonderful step-children, a fantastic mother who is still very much alive and kicking, and three unique and lovely siblings. I am also privileged to "work" in a profession that enables the realization of magnificent potential in others every day.

I have learned that spirituality does not require poverty. The joke is when you surrender to all you can be, allowing yourself to become the best possible version of yourself, when you give yourself this gift, you also give it to all. It tickles me pink that when I evolve myself, I evolve all.

When I stand for truth, it is for everyone. In other words, when I selfishly pursue my own expanded, conscious evolution, I am actually pursuing it for all.

 *Jane MacAllister Dukes*

A PASSION FOR GIVING: THE ANTHONY ROBBINS FOUNDATION
Anthony Robbins

Global Impact
The Anthony Robbins Foundation was created in 1991 with the belief system that, regardless of stature, only those who have learned the power of sincere and selfless contribution experience life's deepest joy: true fulfillment. The Foundation's global impact is provided through an international coalition of caring donors and volunteers who are connecting, inspiring and providing true leadership throughout the world!

Global Relief Efforts
The Anthony Robbins Foundation offers its heartfelt compassion to the victims of the numerous natural disasters felt throughout the world. The Foundation is passionate about participating in the coordination of reconstruction activities and evaluates funding requests on an ongoing basis. As men and women affected by these disasters begin to rebuild, the Anthony Robbins Foundation takes honor in providing hope and funding support to the many suffering communities.

Adopt-A-School Program, New Orleans, USA
Katrina Relief Efforts continue to be a focus of the Foundation. The Foundation will support the rebuilding efforts throughout the Gulf Coast through a partnership with its Youth Mentoring Program partner, Communities In Schools (CIS). CIS is the nation's leading community-based stay-in-school network, connecting needed community resources with schools. CIS has over thirty-four chapters serving well over 2 million children nationally. The Foundation will focus on rebuilding the educational infrastructure currently affecting thousands of children in Louisiana, Mississippi, and Alabama.

The Foundation is proud to announce its partnership with the Adopt-A-School Program in New Orleans to support the rebuilding efforts of

Ben Franklin Elementary. This elementary school was the first public school to open in New Orleans post-Katrina. Ben Franklin Elementary is operating near its capacity by serving 555 students, a 24% increase in student population since Hurricane Katrina. Over 90% of its students reside in high poverty households. The Foundation will provide funding and hands-on assistance toward rebuilding the library, playground and other structural needs. The Foundation's goal is to provide the funds and tools necessary to transform this elementary school into an enhanced learning environment.

Adopt-A-School Program, The Citizens Foundation, Pakistan
The Anthony Robbins Foundation will provide support to The Citizens Foundation which manages many relief programs in Pakistan, rebuilding schools and homes following the earthquake on October 8, 2005. It is widely recognized that, because of crumbling schools, the children suffered the greatest blow from the October quake. It has been reported that some 10,000 schools collapsed throughout Pakistan. The Anthony Robbins Foundation is proud to support the construction of a 6,500 square foot school in the Bagh district of Kashmir, Pakistan. Upon completion, this school will serve 180 students during the academic year beginning in April 2007.

Hebron Orphanage, India
Over the past 40 years, Hebron Orphanage has saved homeless orphans from dying of starvation on the streets of southern India. These orphaned children have been given love, life and a future. The Anthony Robbins Foundation adopted Hebron Orphanage following the 2004 Tsunami. The orphanage has expanded its facilities and now accommodates 400 children. The Foundation is delighted to provide funding to support Hebron Orphanage's immediate need to build a new stand-alone boy's dormitory, enabling the number of male residents to increase to 100, and to allow the current boy's dormitory to be used as a library and classrooms.

Langfang Children's Village, Beijing China

The Langfang Children's Village in Beijing, China was founded to support mainland China's orphaned and special needs children. Many children come to the village because they are abandoned at the front gates or brought to the Langfang by locals. It is home to more than 90 orphans from approximately ten different orphanages scattered throughout China. China is working hard at improving the plight of these children, but as a developing country with over 5 million orphans, the problem is simply too large.

The Langfang Children's Village is designed to model a normal family environment and de-emphasizes the institutional feel often associated with orphanages. Every child lives in a freestanding home with house parents and their own yard to play in. The Anthony Robbins Foundation provides funding to the Langfang Children's Village to support the daily needs of the children as well as medical treatment at an on-location clinic. This collaborative effort is contributing to the well-being of these beautiful children, allowing the Foundation to work toward fulfilling its mission of global impact.

Global Community Connection Day

The Anthony Robbins Foundation proudly sets aside one day a month to proactively connect with non-profit organizations throughout the world. Its goal is to meet the challenges of a global community, come up with solutions and TAKE ACTION! We visit and provide in-kind donations to schools, hospitals, and shelters for the homeless to nurture, feed and mentor those in need. Recently, the Foundation supported the Children's Hospitals of San Diego and New Orleans with donations of stuffed bears for their in-patients. The Foundation also supported the Diabetes Association in their annual Tour de Cure cycling event held in San Diego and Santa Monica, California in honor of the National Physical Fitness and Sports Month.

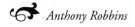

Anthony Robbins

THE KEY TO AN ABUNDANT LIFE
Doug McKee

How we think is really more important than what we think. Until I grasped that simple fact, my life was filled with the drama of never having or being enough. My dreams and goals never seemed to turn out as I hoped or planned. Little did I know, they were turning out exactly as I expected and intended all along.

Like so many others, I had read every self-help and positive-thinking book available. And, as with so many others, my book shelf was the only real recipient of all the important information they contained. Whoever coined the phrase "shelf-help" understood the basic problem humanity has with personal change; no one can make a change in your life except you.

Abundance is an incredibly spiritual and tangible concept that is long overdue in Western thought and practice. We don't realize that we are actually awash in abundance, sometimes so much so that we drown in it.

I can't remember now what made me decide to make a change in my thinking habits for a couple of days, but at the time, it seemed to be a very small step—I doubted much would come of it. I read a book that said it was supposed to radically change the way I would see my world. I was simply to think about all the good things I had in my life and to "count my blessings," as my grandmother was fond of saying. Needless to say, my world changed, and continues to change, in a myriad of ways that are still a marvel to me.

My current understanding and practice of abundance is simple: When we can meet all of our needs, we will then be living an abundant life. That concept isn't difficult, nor are the processes by which we can reach abundance. But there must be something we fail to grasp, either in our understanding or the implementation of the processes, that keeps us from seeing it as such.

The key to an abundant life lies in understanding the difference between needs and wants. Often, the words "need" and "want" are used as synonyms, but their meanings are actually very different. Needs are necessary for growth, development and maintenance. Humans all have the same needs: food, shelter and emotional nurturing (love). To define something as a need is to recognize its essential nature. Words or thoughts cannot satisfy real needs.

A want, on the other hand, is defined as "to fail to have; to be without; to lack." When we want something, we simply don't have it. All of us have worked and slaved for something we thought we wanted, only to find that when we finally got it, it didn't make us a bit happier. Often, satisfying this want only increases our problems. A new house or car that is just a little bit too expensive for our budget, for example, brings the added financial responsibility and worry of having to finance it.

If we analyze carefully and objectively, it is usually not the object we think we desire that is really important to us, but its projected symbolic meaning. The teenage boy doesn't want the car because it is a car. He wants it because it means status, freedom and fun. An object has only the meaning we assign to it from our mental database. We project onto these objects the qualities that we believe we do not have in ourselves. If we get what we think we want, we believe our needs will be met and we will be content and happy.

Attempting to satisfy needs with wants actually hinders us from meeting our real needs. People may eat, shop, exercise or smoke—the possibilities are endless. Since our mental database is designed to accumulate data, substitutions found there will not be correct. We can't eat thoughts or words, and they can't protect us from the weather, so our real needs remain unmet.

This substitution of wants for needs is an attempt to get happiness and peace from the external environment. We all try to convince ourselves that approval of others will lead to happiness. Happiness comes not from attaining desires, but from getting rid of desires for things which cannot meet real needs. Henry David Thoreau knew this when he wrote, "We become prisoners of our possessions." If you have to constantly work hard to pay for something that cannot meet your basic needs, you are a prisoner.

Why have we not learned how to meet our needs? As children, we depended on others to meet most of our needs. It is fairly logical, since they were the source for these needs and didn't teach us otherwise, that we would believe that meeting our needs depends on outside sources. They were also the source for love. This leads us to the conclusion that love is also something external. This is the source of the childhood wound most adults struggle their entire lives to heal. If we don't understand the real nature of needs, we will believe we must depend on an external source to meet them. But this can't work, because you are the only one who can meet your own needs.

Our need-meeting programs are action-based programs, not thinking or information programs. Granted, information is necessary; however, knowledge of how to carry out the action is required to meet the need. Action is the only possible way to meet needs. It does not matter if a person is an infant or 90 years old, everyone has needs and will make efforts to fulfill them.

Most importantly, we must understand that we can meet our needs only by our own actions. If our needs are not being met, we are the only ones who can act to meet them. Someone may bring you food, but you must eat. You may be offered shelter, but you must make the choice to come in out of the rain. Our need for love operates in the same way. When our need for love is met by loving others, our entire world changes dramatically. We each must carry out the action required to meet our needs.

If we will take a brief moment to carefully look at our lives, we will see that they are expressions of abundance. Once we recognize the many blessings we have in our lives, gratitude for our abundance can replace fear of lack. Gratitude removes our mental blocks and allows the universe to fulfill our dreams and desires.

Since I have come to understand how to meet my own needs, my wants are fewer, I am a more loving individual, my relationships are better and gratitude continues to produce ever increasing abundance. May you, too, find your abundance.

 *Doug McKee*

TREASURE MAPPING YOUR WAY TO SUCCESS
Barbara Pellegrino

Either create your life and live your own dreams or
you'll become a pawn in someone else's.

Since 1994, I have been living a life far beyond my wildest dreams!

Who would have imagined that an ordinary girl from Melbourne, Australia, with an ordinary life, would today be living an abundant and extraordinary life, traveling the world with the man of her dreams, living in sun-kissed Hawaii, enjoying life's limitless beauty and teaching her own workshops called "Treasure Mapping Your Way to Success?"

No one believed in my dreams except my mother and me. These days, the rest still shake their heads in amazement and wonder how it all happened. Many still pass it off as luck. Let me tell you a little secret: it was not luck! Ask others who are living their wildest dreams and they will tell you the same thing. Your dreams can happen for you, too.

Achieving your dream requires a certain formula, and the basic ingredients are desire, belief and a clear picture in your mind. Think of your passions, greatest joys and happiness. What are your ideas of total abundance?

We all create our own lives, including our good fortune and abundance. It can happen for you, and you can share it with the people you know and love, so it can happen for them as well.

The three secrets to creating your goals, dreams and desires abundantly, delightfully and easily are TLC:
1) T – Treasure Map. (Vision Board) A visual representation of your goals, dreams and desires.
2) L – Laws. Understanding the universal laws, especially the Law of

Attraction.

3) C – Creation/Manifestation. Learning the art of manifesting.

Sometimes your goals and dreams will come to fruition quickly, and sometimes they may take a little longer, but they always come at the perfect time. By having a completed treasure map on your wall, you will activate the Law of Attraction and fulfill the Art of Manifestation.

Creating your Treasure Map will help you manifest whatever you want in life, because your extremely powerful "creative mind" understands and works in pictures. Looking at your map will trigger your passions and give your mind focus and clarity. Therefore, your subconscious mind becomes programmed like a guided missile aimed at your goals and dreams, instead of just dwelling on and recreating your past!

Your Treasure Map is a visual representation of what you want your future to become, just as you have photos of your past successes on your walls at home. You will now have a map with clear and definite pictures that will direct your creative mind in manifesting your future.

Your history does not have to repeat itself! Your past is not your future. Turn around, look at your dreams, and move forward now.

You might say, "I already have written goals." That's great for the left side of your brain, but what about the right side—the creative side? Adding the visuals is a more powerful way to set your goals and achieve the dreams and abundance you want. The only limits are your level of desire and your willingness to act.

The map I made in 1994 is still bringing me great joy and wonderful adventures, and I create new maps regularly to add to my fabulous and abundantly happy life.

You will find the journey toward your dreams will become more of an adventure of discovery; like finding treasures buried along the way that may require some effort to uncover. At other times, they are just waiting to be found and appear to be a coincidence.

All disciplines teach that we create our own reality by the thoughts we think, the feelings we have and the pictures we make in our minds. Current scientific research is beginning to support the timeless belief that thoughts are real forces, and it's through our thoughts that we experience our life. Therefore, you are creating your own reality in every moment. Quantum physics have proven that everything is energy. The smallest particles of solid matter (called quarks) in a table or a rock or a person are just energy vibrating at the sub-atomic level.

Every thought and feeling you experience is energy—a frequency like a magnet that attracts similar thoughts and feelings. It's true for all people, all places, all of the time. The Law of Attraction states that the situations and circumstances of your life will be a reflection of your predominant thoughts and feelings. After a certain amount of time, they will manifest into your reality.

No wonder people find themselves in so many mixed circumstances. It appears to be good luck and bad luck, but it's only the universe responding to your predominant thoughts and feelings. The positives, the negatives, the worries, the desires and the pictures are all mixed up, as they are in an untrained, unfocused mind.

In the movie *The Secret*, the Law of Attraction is depicted as a giant genie, and all it says is, "Your wish is my command." The universe does not grant wishes. It works impartially and unemotionally, just like gravity. It doesn't judge your character or decide if you deserve your dreams. It doesn't manifest a fleeting wish, it only responds to what it continuously receives.

Like attracts like, and whatever thoughts and feelings are held firm and strong will materialize; "As you sow, you shall reap!"

A Treasure Map aligns all the aspects of your creative and powerful mind—your imagination, intuition, conscious and subconscious mind, thoughts, feelings and passions—which then guide your actions. What more could you want? Uniting all of your parts is the most powerful thing you can do for yourself. They make an awesome team!

When you begin your quest for living the life you love and create your Treasure Map, you are taking the first powerful step in having the life you desire. Then the universe moves quickly toward you and is ready to shower abundance upon you in the form of the dreams, pictures and goals you see on your map. You are the alchemist of your life, so you get to design the life you want to live.

The minimum requirement for manifestation with a Treasure Map is simply looking at your map occasionally. To produce quick results, look at it often and imagine the pictures you see are already real. Fill your powerful mind with thoughts and feelings of celebration, joy, happiness and gratitude toward God, or your personal spiritual source.

Three percent of the world's highest achievers have firm, recorded goals. The next 10 percent have goals in mind. The rest of the world's population has empty wishes and hopes. They rely on luck or good fortune to make their dreams come true. For the vast majority, it never happens.

In what section of the population do you currently reside, and where would you like to be? All you have to do is act now! Now is the best time to create your Treasure Map and place yourself among the top three percent. Then, enjoy the abundance!

 *Barbara Pellegrino*

ALL ABUNDANCE IS WITHIN YOU
Dan Hanneman

All the treasures of life are already within us; we simply need to open up the doors within our beings to allow the life we love to flow through us. Your creator has already given you all the perfect health, wealth, inspiration, talent, peace, harmony and joy that you desire; it is implanted within your soul. Once we become aware of our soul's highest desire for our life, we begin to open the doors within our being to allow for the connection and expression of the total abundance that is already within ourselves.

What is your soul's highest desire? Are you connecting and expressing it in your daily life? We have all had times in our lives when we have been connected with it, whether consciously or unconsciously. Often it is the memories of our childhood that will show us what we loved doing before we allowed other things to distract us. We all have that seed of magnificence and wellness within our soul that wishes to blossom into our lives.

When I was a child, I had a passion for being creative, for writing, for guiding others and for being an entrepreneur. It was my lack of trust in this connection and what I could accomplish in these areas that led my life adrift during my adolescence and early adulthood. I became very depressed and withdrawn during my high school and early college years. There was always a part of me that knew that there was something fabulous inside me that wanted to be expressed, but my mind limited my possibilities because of the anxiety at the thought of sharing myself with other people. My fears told me that others would reject me. I could have decided to blame societal or parental conditioning, but there was a part of me that knew I was responsible for my life and how I was feeling. It was the part of me that kept me coming back to focus on creative writing, journaling and exercising that helped give me that connection of wellness within my being once again.

My ultimate transformation occurred when I became clear on what would help me break free from depression and began to align my daily actions with what would bring me joy. I wanted to help others do the same, so I went on to major in psychology. After graduating, I took a side-step by going into outside sales in order to further confront my fear of rejection and to satisfy the desire to connect with the lives of others. Although I was experiencing personal growth and building people skills, it was not a completely satisfying endeavor for me—I knew there was something missing. After going on to get my master's degree in clinical psychology, I went on to work in the mental health field, feeling blessed to be able to change people's lives. I now have my own private practice in which I offer hypnotherapy, counseling and spiritual life coaching. I am also an author, speaker and trainer; I teach others to live life to the fullest by finding their soul's highest desire and taking bold, inspired action. I have additional business plans that will cumulatively result in a multi-million dollar enterprise that will help others to clearly see what they desire in their life and give them pathways to reach their highest levels of fulfillment. It has been quite a journey to get where I am today. The discovery of my soul's highest desire determines every step in my life. This desire is to touch people with a consciousness of the love that connects us all, in order to unlock the gifts, talents and capacities within each person. There is actually no endpoint in this journey; rather, it is an ongoing experience of joy being expressed through me in each moment along the way.

You may ask, "How, then, do I discover my soul's highest desire?" Although there may be a number of ways to make this discovery, I have found that using a visioning process, which was adapted from Dr. Michael Beckwith's work, to be a most effective way. Here are some of the basic steps in the process that you can begin to utilize within your own life:

1. Go to a quiet place in your physical environment and in your mind. Have paper and pencil ready.

2. Begin by affirming your connection with the infinite intelligence of God/the universe that exists within all life.

3. Affirm that God/the universe is bringing into your awareness all the wisdom needed in your life through this visioning process.

4. You recognize God's intelligence is within you and you are receptive to your soul's highest desire.

5. Begin to ask questions such as: What is God/the universe's highest vision for my life? What must I become to empower this vision? What must I let go of to empower this vision? Give yourself a few moments to listen for messages to emerge in response to each question. Be careful to allow the answers to surface, and ask, "What does this mean?" if you are feeling puzzled. The messages will emerge from your subconscious mind in the way of pictures, words, colors and other impressions. These will not come to you through conscious control. Simply trust what emerges without judgment, knowing that it is all absolutely perfect.

It is through this visioning process, daily meditation and affirmations, setting vision-led goals, and taking bold, inspired, daily action that every aspect of your life will begin to transform. You will discover a feeling of peace and abundance that is at the core of your being. When you trust the process of this unfolding of your being (as you do when planting a seed in your garden), you can live from a place of trust and love in your heart, knowing that everything is springing forth perfectly in your life. You want to make it your practice to enjoy, love and give gratitude at every step along your life's journey. I want you to fully recognize that the abundance and blessings of life are already within you. As you remain thankful and expect good to manifest in your outer life, you provide an ideal environment for a blissful and abundant life as each moment unfolds. Within you, you already have all you desire in life; it is just waiting for your conscious connection with it. As your connection deepens with your inner being, your soul's highest desire will become clearer to you. Once you completely trust what you are connecting with inside your soul, then you will become inspired to follow through on what is nudging you to experience total prosperity in both the spiritual and physical realm of your life. You are good enough and you can do it. Start today!

 Dan Hanneman

IN SERVICE TO THE CHILDREN
Kay Snow-Davis

You are invited to be alive through the light and the love of the child—the child in you, the child that you parent, the grandchild that you cherish, the unseen child in all life.

You were born in innocence and pureness and are sustained daily by that power and presence. All of your life experiences have generated the strength, courage and commitment it takes to live a human life. If your human life was not surrounded by your soul, transmitting life to your heart, relayed by the breath to each cell, you would not be alive.

Aliveness is not an emotion. It is an agreement that generates experiences of movement, change and unity with all life. Recall the last time you felt alive. That is the feeling that lives within you, waiting release as your lifestyle. You are not lost, you never have been. The child in you is your aliveness. Did you lose your child? Your child has never lost you and never will. The only way for you to experience "losing your child" is through mental beliefs and illusions that create a sense of separation from your heart and soul. Your heart and soul are the eternal home for your child.

Aliveness is an inside job. You can see it, feel it and experience it in your heart and soul. Aliveness is reflected in all of nature, which is free of the distortion. The human mind, in a moment of amnesia, created the illusion of judgment, generating a belief of being separated from the divine order of the universe. When you make an agreement, consciously or unconsciously, being imprisoned by judgment diminishes your aliveness.

You can change your agreement and commit to aliveness. Now is the moment. You do not need to go anywhere, read any book, see any movie, study to be worthy, or "work" to overcome your inadequacies. Just be still. In this moment, gently turn your view inside and feel your heart and give yourself permission to "see" that precious child that awaits your recognition. Be still and feel the love that you are through this child. Receive the love. Embrace your child. Breathe.

When you are ready, slowly turn and face the world, the one that appears outside of your heart. What do you feel? What do you see? From this moment on, united with the child of your heart and soul, your experience of life will never be the same.

In innocence and curiosity, you can now enter the world anew, experiencing life at a level of truth—a level that is not available veiled through the illusion of separation, judgment, guilt or shame. Though these innocent eyes, you are now viewing life from your heart.

You can see the world as your heart knows it to be. From that perception, you can make choices that are congruent and harmonious with your soul. United with your child, you are the living expression of love in action.

We are the children—every age, every gender, every nationality, every culture, and every tradition. We are the future.

 *Kay Snow-Davis*

A DIARY OF "WAKING UP"
Suria Mohd

This is a diary of how I went from heavy debt and having less than $50 in my bank account to running two six-figure businesses in one year's time, and it all started when I decided to *"Wake Up and Live the Life I Love!"*

My reality on July 10, 2003:
On that fateful day, I was desperately crying for help when I stumbled upon a Web site that prompted me to ask myself key questions about my life. With some guided inspiration, I took actions that were to be the turning points in my life.

Step 1: I listed what was happening at that moment—positive and negative, wanted and unwanted—just the facts of my present circumstances.

Confessions of my reality on July 10, 2003:
I'm dead broke. I owe five banks and have a failing business with rent due. I have no time to spend with my children and I feel lousy.

The good thing is I'm still hanging on. At times like this, I only have my dreams to hang on to. That is my only hope.

Step 2: I listed the thoughts about my current reality; my opinions, my judgments, evaluations and comments—whether positive or negative—about what was happening in my life at that moment.

My confessions:
My concerns are the legal implications if I cannot settle my debts. It does not feel right that I have no time with my children, despite the fact I am not working.

Step 3: I listed my emotions—mad, sad or glad; upset or angry; excited or bored; numb or alive; good or bad.

My emotional confessions:
I am far from feeling happy. I feel desperate. I need money to save my business. I am upset that I don't see my kids enough; I feel I have failed as a mother.

Yet, deep down, my optimism and my desire to make things happen in life still can't defeat my feelings of failure. I still look at life positively and see some light; what light, I don't know. I see much opportunity to create a successful business, yet I'm not making it.

Step 4: I asked myself how I was feeling physically; was I relaxed or tense? Did I feel any pain or discomfort?

My physical body confessions:
I feel tired and I am not functioning at my optimal level. I feel weak and listless.

Step 5: I rated my profile in terms of what I wanted and didn't want; 10 meaning "Exactly what I want" and one meaning "What I don't want my life to be like."

My rating confessions:
My ratings were a 4. Many things were not right: the way I lived, the way I spent time with my kids, my whole life in general.

Step 6: I created my vision. *The words stared me in the face: Express your desire right now, use your imagination to create a Level 10 life. Create a movie script describing all that is happening. Use only positive present tense, no negatives. Describe things as if they are happening right now.*

My confessions from my movie script—Lights...Camera...Action...
I have $4,000 in my bank account right now and I'm transferring all of the money to my debts. I will pay the bills in $500 installments. I feel a great sense of relief and I am so glad I have conquered this huge mountain in my life.

I get up early to take the kids to the playground; we go to the beach and play until noon. I bring them home, we eat lunch and then I'm off to work. I feel so glad to be able to spend time with the kids. I am so happy as a mother. I feel so complete today.

I plan to take up my business and create targeted action plans. I am clear on my goals; I know what I want and know the actions required to get there.

Step 7: I listed the thoughts I had—any positive opinions, judgments, evaluations—about my vision using present tense and positive, affirming thoughts.

My confessions of my thoughts and opinions of my vision:
I feel so clear, so rich, so content. I feel so grown, so experienced, so powerful with all that I've accomplished and faced.

Step 8: I listed the positive emotions I was feeling—upbeat, high-energy, loving, happy, peaceful and joyful.

My confessions of my emotional state:
I feel relaxed as I envision the possibilities of making such things happen. I feel that I have to step back and really put in writing what I need to do step-by-step to cut my losses and revive the business. This makes me feel secure.

Step 9: I asked myself, "How do I feel now, physically? Are they good feelings?" I listed only the good—no pains or sad victim stories.

My final confessions:
I feel more relaxed now as I see myself achieving success by doing the things I planned to do.
Whew! Completing the exercise made me feel like a truckload of sand-bags had been lifted from my shoulders. I just don't know how all those would have unfolded themselves. At least it happened in my tiny,

experimental laboratory space called "my mind." Whatever it was, I loved the ideas that were created.

This is the way I intend for my life to be. I surrender and submit to the highest power to allow everything to happen naturally and effortlessly and for the highest good of myself and all concerned to be achieved.

After I "woke up," incidents in life prompted me to take mini-actions that led to my current success. As a nutritionist and educator, I have a deep, ingrained passion to teach nutrition and to help people lose weight. Educating and transforming lives through the power of the spoken word is in my blood. It's what I love, live and breath for.

Once, I agreed to help a local health club by giving a speech to its members. This increased my Nutrition and Weight Management engagements from one to hundreds of talks, from corporate organizations to government agencies. I started teaching the public how they could lose weight without starving themselves while living in an Asian food haven. Soon after, I did radio interviews, wrote articles for magazines and even appeared on some magazine covers. I was also included on an expert panel on one of the most popular weight loss reality shows.

I woke up when I took that first step to audit my current reality and started creating these mental images in my mind. I learned not to ask how, but rather to just believe in the outcomes, and then natural coincidences nudged me toward mini-steps to success. It took action, but it all started from a simple belief.

If I were to sum up everything into four words, they would be:

BELIEF—THOUGHTS—ACTIONS—RESULTS

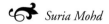 *Suria Mohd*

THE TIME OF OUR LIVES
Rebecca Grado

Some people define abundance as having material wealth—overflowing bank accounts or oodles of "toys," like nice cars, big houses and expensive jewelry. For me, though, abundance is measured in more than money or possessions. An abundant life is one in which I am free to do what I want, when I want; no restrictions, deadlines or schedules.

There is nothing more appealing to me than waking up, knowing that the day is mine to create exactly as I choose. If I want to stay snuggled up in bed with a good book and a warm cup of coffee, that's up to me. If I would rather throw on some sweats and hike around the hills by my home with my black lab, Joey, then that works, too. For me, knowing that I am completely free to create the life I desire is the truest definition of abundance.

A few years ago, I did something out of the ordinary. I bought a recreational vehicle, packed up my two kids (then, ages 9 and 13)—and Joey, too—and off we went. We hit the road for a three-year, 48-state adventure across the good old USA. Crazy, you say? Well that's exactly what everyone else said—including the voice inside my own head.

But you know what? During that time of exploration (and sometimes exasperation), celebration of the beauty of our country and deep connection to my kids, I was the most alive I have ever felt. Although we didn't have material abundance, and the lifestyle was definitely not posh, what we did have was a profound abundance of freedom, adventure, peace of mind and wonderful memories. Every day felt like a blessing, and there were many moments of pure wonder.

So what led me to conceive this crazy idea? Several things led up to it, but it was mainly a feeling that life was passing me by and I didn't want to miss the most precious years of my kids' lives by getting caught up with my "to-do" lists.

Before embarking on this road trip, we were just a typical family. I was a single mom juggling my psychotherapy practice and keeping up with school schedules and play dates, Tae Kwon Do classes and ballet lessons. As much as I adored my kids and cherished my time with them, the truth is I was getting bored. I was feeling bogged down in the routine and the constant demand on my time. I kept wondering, "Is this it? Is this as good as it gets?"

In moments of clarity, I could see that we were "falling asleep" and missing out on the great adventure of our lives. We were succumbing to the hypnotic trance of going through the motions in suburbia—the kids went to school all day, came home and did their homework or went to various lessons or sport practices, ate dinner and went to sleep. Weekends were relegated to lawn mowing, warehouse shopping and more sports events. Just slap a sticker boasting "Proud Parent of an Honor Student" to the bumper of our SUV and call us "asleep at the wheel!"

Now, I've always been a bit of a free spirit—as are my kids—and we did our fair share of vacations, traveling and general merry mayhem, but these were brief moments of wakefulness before getting back to the doldrums of our routines. It wasn't that I was locked into a horrendous commute or a 9-to-5 job—I have a home office and I make my own hours—yet, I still felt stifled and constrained by schedules and routines. Where was our adventurous spirit? Where was our enthusiasm for life and our eagerness to greet each day? Who says we have to learn in a classroom and earn our money in an office?

It saddens me to think of all the people who have lost sight of their personal dreams and have relinquished their lives to the mundane. I work with so many clients who are withdrawn, depressed, anxious, unfulfilled and empty, and they don't know why. It scares me to think how dangerously close I came to missing out on my own life. So, although this notion of hitting the wide-open road may sound far fetched, crazy or even irresponsible, it was truly the most liberating decision I have ever made. I chose to take charge of my life and free my family from the mindless day-to-day existence into which we had fallen.

Choosing to write a different script for my family certainly wasn't easy, and life on the road came with its own set of challenges. Did I have fears, doubts, worry, free-floating anxiety or moments of sheer hysteria? Sure; every day. But I didn't allow myself to give into these fears or allow them to dictate the direction of our lives.

We saw each day as an amazing gift, one that was to be cherished and appreciated—not wasted in apathy and drudgery. We greeted each day with our arms open wide, ready to receive all the adventures life had to offer. We were free and our lives were full. I can't tell you how many incredible experiences we've had. We have been to glaciers and temperate rainforests, majestic canyons and breathtaking coasts. We've been up close and personal with alligators in the Everglades and grizzly bears in Montana. We've enjoyed sugar shacks in Vermont, lobster shacks in Maine, Mardi Gras in New Orleans and Native American reservations in New Mexico. We've toured all the state capitals, from tiny Rhode Island to mighty Texas, and we've learned how things are made in factories all over the country. Every day was new, exciting and immensely abundant. Our prosperity came in the form of opportunities, experiences, blessings and a deep connection to one another.

I am not saying it's necessary to trade in your lifestyle for an RV in order to reap life's blessings or embrace each day with enthusiasm; this was just my outlet. What I now encourage others to do is to find their blessings and prosperity in those qualities that really matter. I often ask myself how I would spend my time if I only had a year (or month, week, or day) to live. Would my choices and priorities be different? I will tell you that building my fortune, cleaning the house or running errands never top my list anymore. Since being home, my deepest desire is to truly enjoy each moment as it comes and to connect deeply with those I love.

My life on the road has taught me that what matters most and what brings me peace of mind has very little to do with achieving, accomplishing or acquiring material possessions. Abundance is about simply being free and enjoying your life!

 Rebecca Grado

UNLEASH THE POWERFUL PROMOTER WITHIN
Matt Bacak

Dear Friend,

You're ripping me off.

"How?" you may be thinking. "We just met. How could I possibly have stolen from you?"

The fact is that you have valuable information inside you. You have golden nuggets that can make lives better. Maybe you have already developed them into products, services or seminars. If you do not market your gold, how will anyone know? You must then persuade people to buy and use them because people are overwhelmed with options. If you don't make your wisdom available, you are hurting them.

I don't care if it's a security alarm, a beauty product, financial service, a business opportunity or anything else. Your knowledge, product or service could be helping people solve their problems. And if it can't help people, why are you doing it in the first place?

So many times I see people out there and they have the best product on the market. But it's sitting on their shelf in storage or it's still in their heads and they're not telling anyone about it. At the very same time, their competitors (with inferior products and less to offer) are selling to people and hurting them. Inferiority hurts.

Awhile back, I learned a huge lesson: If you plant bad seeds, you get a bad harvest. Well, it's time to start planting good seeds and lots of them.

Because you never shared your unique knowledge and products with me, you ripped me off. Not only did you rip me off, but you ripped off all those you could have shared your message with. Quite possibly, you have ripped off the world! It's your job, your duty, to share and persuade people to use your services and products. Discover how to market your products—get them out there!

On top of all that, you ripped yourself off because you're not putting the money you deserve into your own pockets. Change the world, especially your own.

 *Matt Bacak*

As Dusk Approached
Stephen A. Burgess

Sometimes it takes a tragedy to discover the real meaning of life. Such was the case with my friend Tony.

Tony was an everyday kind of guy—working hard and doing his best to provide for his family. Tony was a wonderful husband and father, and spent his time with his family.

Tony always had a smile on his face. He would help anyone he met, even a stranger. If he knew you needed help painting your house or fixing your car, he was the first to volunteer. He played on our soccer team but was the last player to be chosen for the team. That didn't bother Tony. He cheered us on relentlessly. When he did get a few minutes on the field, he played with all his energy and his famous smile.

Tony took a fishing trip with his son and another father and son. They went to a small stream that was only waist deep; they could float down as they fished. It was a beautiful day with the sun shining and the wildlife roaming the shores. They caught a few fish and had a picnic. They all told jokes and laughed. It was just the two fathers and their sons sharing a wonderful day.

As dusk approached, Tony and his friend picked out a spot where they could stop the boat. Then it happened. Without warning, the boat struck something and flipped, dumping all four of them into the frigid water. The other father found his footing and jumped up, gasping for air. He quickly looked around and saw his son, partially submerged. He grabbed him and struggled to catch his breath as he pulled his son to shore.

Tony had also found his footing and came up, gasping for air. When Tony looked around, he could not see his son and called his name in desperation. There wasn't a response. Despite the icy cold, he felt his way around the overturned boat to try to find his son, but there was nothing. Tony took a deep breath and dove headfirst under the boat looking for his son, but it was in vain. He came up gasping as the icy water sapped his strength. He wouldn't give up. He dove under again and again but could not find his son. As he came up gasping the final time, little did he know that his son was only feet away, caught by the submerged limb that had overturned the boat. Both were lost that day.

When I went to their funeral, I was deeply touched by the grief of his wife and daughter. The eulogist told stories about Tony, reminding us of his tremendous spirit and sense of humor. We smiled at many of them. Then he said something amazing, "Tony was the richest, most successful man I ever met."

I thought, "Tony wasn't rich." But the speaker said, "Look around you. This church holds 500, but there are 750 people packed in here and another 250 outside. All of you are here because Tony touched your lives. He gave something to each of you and never asked for anything in return. I cannot think of a better example of success or a person who lived a richer life."

I realized he was right. The greatest purpose any of us can have is to live like Tony, to give to others without reservation, to help others in any way we can. Twenty years later, we still talk about Tony. We remember what he gave to each of us and what he taught us through his life.

He truly was a rich and successful man.

Stephen A. Burgess

Play the Game!
Kerron "Ron" Wilson

When I was in college, people often asked what sport I played, and to their disappointment, I would say, "None." The truth, however, was that I was playing the game we all play—the game of life. You get certain results based on your participation in the game. If you participate a little, you get little results; if you participate a lot, you again get the corresponding results. So I decided that the best way to be successful is to practice, as is the case in all games. I liken this to a football player; he doesn't practice just for the sake of practicing, he practices for the sake of being the best player possible. He practices with a purpose; anything else is just a waste of time. It is the same with human beings—we should all practice to be the best person possible. The attributes that a person must practice at to be great are ones we all have—we often just fail to exercise them. The attributes that determine where any person will end up in life are attitude, motivation, desire and confidence.

Your attitude is a wonderful tool because—unlike your personality, which usually doesn't change throughout your lifetime—your attitude can change no matter what life throws your way. Your attitude is like the genie in Aladdin's lamp—whatever you ask or wish it to do, it does without question. To cultivate a positive attitude, surround yourself with individuals who have positive attitudes. The same can be said of motivation, desire and confidence. Just try it, and I guarantee you will see a change in every facet of your life. You are who you walk with, so be great by walking with great people. If you can't walk with great people, then learn to serve great people. In doing so, you become great by default. When all is said and done, you want your friends to remember you as someone who inspired others to do greater things than they ever dreamed possible—you want them to remember you were great because you were not afraid to walk with giants.

Desire and motivation are the two engines that drive every accomplishment in life. When I teach, I often say, "I can give you all the tools in the world to be successful, but I cannot manufacture desire and motivation—that is something you have to come to the table with. If you don't have them, then you must find a way to create them in your life on a daily basis."

Here are a few tips on creating an assembly line for motivation and desire:

Tip Number One: Ask yourself why you are doing whatever it is you are currently doing. Does it add value to someone else? You or your business can only grow if others grow. Remember: We can all be wealthy if we only learn to invest in each other. Zig Ziglar is famous for the quotation, "If you help enough people get what they want, you can have everything that you want."

Tip Number Two: Look at your life and appreciate the good that is present, because there is always something to be grateful for. A great leader finds the positive in every negative. Master that, and every wall that you encounter will fall at your feet.

Tip Number Three: Do not accept life as what it is; accept it as what it can become. Always move forward, because water that does not flow eventually kills everything it comes in contact with; even a river finds its way to the ocean. Every day, become more than you were the previous day, and that can be as simple as learning a new word or concept.

Finally, let's talk about confidence. We have all heard the saying, "If you don't use it, you will lose it." The same can be said about confidence. Think of your confidence as a muscle—the more you exercise or build it, the stronger it becomes. You may only have a penny in your pocket, but your confidence is worth millions. Face it—we love to do business with confident people because their confidence in what they are offering gives us confidence in the item as well. Take a look in your closet and you will see many items you bought that you never have and never will use—they are just taking up space. However, a confident individual got you to see value in the items and you bought them. Confidence is contagious.

Here are a few tips for boosting your confidence: Dress for success— wear the best suit, dress, shoes, attitude and smile at all times (I love working with happy people). Next, talk to yourself like a cheerleader; look in the mirror and tell yourself in a positive, confirming and commanding tone that you are confident, and it will be so, because whatever you think of yourself, others will think also. Do this ritual as often as possible. Next, help build up the confidence of others, and you will be surrounded in a utopia of confident people—and you will increase the chances that people will like you.

Showing up does not guarantee that you will get paid, but it helps. Learn to show up in all you do—your attitude, motivation, desire and confidence. If you do these simple things, success will be yours for the taking.

Hanging with the eagles doesn't guarantee that you will fly, but it will increase your chances.

 *Kerron "Ron" Wilson*

LIVE LIFE TO THE FULLEST BECAUSE YOU NEVER KNOW
Heissam Jebailey

I was born in Canada and lived there until I was five, then moved to the states with my very loving, but strict, Lebanese family—one in which drinking and smoking were prohibited, and dating was forbidden until you were ready for marriage. At least that's how I thought it was—until I turned 21. After that, my parents became more open-minded and allowed me, my two brothers and my sister to venture out and do more than in years past.

Unlike my parents and siblings, I was quite a worrier and went through grade school, high school and college by working hard and stressing throughout most of it. I never missed a single day or a homework assignment. If I got sick, I'd still go to school; if I accidentally skipped a page in my workbook, I'd freak out. I even had an imaginary friend that would question every little thing I did. As if my worrying and stressing wasn't enough, I had someone who didn't even exist putting additional pressure on me. I was always thinking far too much about the most insignificant things, wondering "what if this" and "what if that." The stress put a damper on my life as a whole, but I just couldn't help it. Simply put, I did not enjoy my younger days as much as I should have.

While growing up, I was very much loved and respected as a student and person. I'd like to think that I had a lot of friends, although I never got into the whole high school and college scene of partying, staying out late and enjoying life outside of school like the other students. My free time in college consisted of very little social activity, as I was working and studying to gain experience for the real world. I took classes full-time and held multiple internships and jobs all four years. This obviously didn't leave much time to enjoy anything else that might have come my way—hobbies, friends, entertainment or adventure.

Within a month of graduation I received a great job working for a college newspaper. I have to admit that all that hard work paid off. From my first day on the job—much like my life thus far—I put my heart and soul into it and nothing else. I worked day and night shifts for a full year. And if I thought I had stressed and worried before graduation, I was now making a career of it. I worked so intensely during that first year that I neglected to eat right and sleep well. I was in a difficult relationship and continued to overwork and over-think until, one evening, my life flashed before my eyes.

At only 22 years old, I was rushed to a nearby hospital with a 105 degree fever, severe chills and more scared than ever before. An x-ray showed that one half of my lungs were filled with water. I was sent home with antibiotics, and for the first time in my life I had to call in sick to work five days straight. I still couldn't eat or sleep and I realized something was severely wrong. My parents took me to our family doctor who said that if I didn't admit myself to the emergency room soon, my life would end.

I wouldn't wish this experience on my worst enemy. At that time, another x-ray showed that both my lungs were filled with water, signifying a deadly case of pneumonia which was close to cutting off my air supply. The next month included needles, x-rays and various tests. I had to have a new x-ray every day and underwent several oral surgeries because the doctors could not figure out how to cure me at that point. Our priest came in to say a prayer, and that's when I realized my life might be over.

To me, the bad news was that if I died then, I would have nothing fun to show for it, and all the worrying and stressing I had undergone simply hadn't been worth it. The good news was that the love and care I received from everyone I knew and didn't know was just one aspect of what eventually saved me. That's when you know you are really appreciated.

Finally, two of the best surgeons in the world performed an intensive lung surgery. Although it left a permanent 10-inch scar and daily reminder on my back, it also saved my life. After the anesthesia wore off and I found myself extremely grateful to still be alive, I promised myself that I would do whatever it took to work reasonably, to eliminate my worries, and to stress as little as possible in order to live life to the fullest from that day forward. I also wanted to teach others not to make the same mistakes I had. Now I share my story with college students so I can remind them to enjoy their experiences; I want them not only to become successful, but to continuously strive to enjoy and appreciate life.

Looking back, I truly believe that without the abundance of help and love I received from God, family and friends from all over the world, I wouldn't be here today. Since that dreadful but eye-opening incident, I've been blessed with having been an owner and operator of a newspaper while building a commercial real estate company and college speaking career on the side. I've traveled the world and enjoyed life as never before. I learned the hard way that achievement through stress and neglect of your health is not worthwhile. Without your health, everything else means nothing.

Does any part of your life seem like my early days? If so, then I urge you to "wake up" to the abundance around you. It's beautiful!

 *Heissam Jebailey*

Love Yourself Enough to Live a Healthy Life
Lyne Simons

In 1989, I received a blow to the head from a light fixture that fell two stories, knocking me out while I was sitting in a seminar on a ship in Long Beach, California. I had a concussion, dizziness, tinnitus and short-term memory loss. I was diagnosed with post-traumatic stress syndrome and became very fearful and depressed. I began stuttering and losing my train of thought. I was later told I was very lucky that I hadn't ended up in a coma or with any paralysis.

I thought my career as a speaker was over. I was forced to slow down, stop and be quiet for long periods of time. For the next 12 years, I lived a life of quiet desperation, trying to pretend all was as it used to be. My physical and emotional health on a fast downward spiral, I tried to pretend I was as good as ever, fooling no one but myself. At one point, my feelings of worthlessness were so bad that I attempted suicide.

It's amazing how years of avoiding emotional issues can catch up with you in illness and stillness! I began a slow—and often painful—inward journey, searching for what my life's purpose might be and why this had happened to me.

My turning point came when I heard how my friend, Carolyn Wunderlich, had turned her life around with a marvelous new system involving cleansing and good nutrition. She had been diagnosed with a life threatening liver condition which she was able to reverse through this amazing method, without the recommended surgery. When I first heard her courageous story, I was overweight, without energy and having joint pain and headaches. I couldn't wait to see what this cutting edge technology could do for me.

The immediate changes in my life were nothing short of miraculous! After 30 days, I was so enthusiastic about sharing it with my friends and family that I overcame my embarrassment enough to reveal some really remarkable, but personal, life changes. During the first nine days I lost 12 pounds and 15 inches. I found this so remarkable I posted a before and after picture, with my fat belly hanging over my swimsuit, because I looked so different in the after shot!

As I traded my poor eating habits for healthy ones, I started waking up each day with increased energy and vigor. What I didn't tell even some of my closest friends was that after 30 days on this marvelous new and easy nutritional system, I had secretly quit taking my depression medication and my hormone pills. Yet, I didn't have any more hot flashes or night sweats. My brain felt like a fog had been cleared out and my memory began to work so much better.

My fear and depression are finally gone. I feel that I can handle whatever life sends my way without going to bed and pulling the covers over my head. After 12 years on antidepressants, this alone has been life changing for me.

As a side benefit of cleansing my liver, my age spots have disappeared. My skin is softer and less wrinkled after hydrating my body with 64 ounces of water a day. After feeding my body with good nutrients, my hair is growing in thicker and shinier and my nails are growing long and healthy for the first time in 20 years! My 35-year addiction to Coca-Cola is over. I have no more cravings for candy, ice cream or chocolate.

Most remarkable to me is that as I shed the toxins from my body, I am also able to release those toxic emotions of self-loathing, anger, hatred and fear that I had stored in my heart and spirit for so long. I am healthier and look younger than I did 10 years ago.

I now know that millions of people with chronic illnesses, such as metabolic syndrome, can improve their quality of life with my system. Dr. Paul Berns, a Beverly Hills internist who specializes in integrative medicine and emphasizes good nutrition, supports my nutritional program.

He states, "I have seen many patients lower their blood pressure, improve their lipid abnormalities and increase their general strength and vitality by a nutritional lifestyle change."

There is an incredible lightness to my being now. At the risk of sounding overly dramatic, I feel as if I am now living more like what God intended when he created me. My body functions with grace and ease again, and my spirit soars each day. I truly feel as if I have been released from a cage and am completely alive now. I have such joy and happiness when I wake up each day and feel such love for my new healthy self and for others. I am a woman with a mission, and it is no longer "mission impossible." I believe that I am now living part of my life's purpose when I tell others about this amazing Isagenix technology. I find I can be myself, love myself and even like the self I am!

Using this remarkable system has changed my body, mind, spirit and life! I love showing others how they can open their hearts, minds and bodies to good health and happiness.

In the universe of all time, you are the only you. Love yourself enough to be truly healthy and alive as you live a life you love!

 *Lyne Simons*

THE PROOF YOU NEED
LaTanya White

I've heard of people finding—or, rather, looking for—the answers to their problems at the bottom of a bottle, but I never knew it would be so rewarding and fulfilling for me to do so. Despite my status as a mixologist and professional bartender, my intention is not to make an alcoholic out of my patrons and neither do I promote alcoholism. Go back with me to a time not so long ago, if you will, and I'll tell you what I mean.

I was only 26 years old when I married the man that I had been seriously involved with my entire adult life—the man I was sure I would spend the rest of my life with. I was 27 when we separated and 28 when the divorce became final. In the months before he put his hands around my neck, things between us were already reaching a point of absolute no return. It was about a week or so after his fingerprints faded away that he decided that it was imperative for me to leave our apartment and he called the police to escort me out. The police came and the officer informed me that I did not have to leave, but I wonder, had I stayed, would I be here to share my story with you today? It was the proof I needed in order to accept that my marriage was over.

In retrospect, I now see how much of me had truly been sacrificed in my efforts to make that six-year relationship work. My friends, my family, my passions, my desires—the things that used to be so important to the fiber of my being and the fabric of my character—had been alienated. The unfamiliarity of it all brought about a certain comfort though; so comfortable, in fact, that I did not realize how estranged I had become from the people and things that had been near to my heart, until one of my uncles said to me, "Welcome back," about a month after my husband and I separated. Wow! I had to be welcomed back to my own family because of how strategically I had separated myself.

In the activities that positioned me for rediscovery of my self, I became very involved with my sorority and forged relationships with many of my sorority sisters, who I hadn't previously been able to open myself up to. One of my line sisters was in the planning stages of her birthday party and asked that I bartend it for her. In my short time on this earth, I have been asked by many people to do many things, but this was by far the most random. I committed to her request on the condition that I not be held accountable if the guests were not satisfied with their drinks. I don't know how Sara drew the conclusion that I was qualified to assist her guests in their activities of imbibing. I mean, I had thought about bartending before but I don't recall ever mentioning that to her. When I was a sophomore in college, I had looked into attending the bartending school that was being advertised in the campus paper, but in 1998, to a student working at the local chicken shack, $300 was far too steep an investment. So, that dream was deferred very early in its developmental stages.

On the evening of the party, I debated fulfilling the commitment I had obligated myself to. I was in the mood to feel sorry for myself, wondering how I had ruined my marriage. And now, over a year later, I still have no idea why I wasn't the woman he turned out to be in love with. But I sucked it up and headed to the restaurant where the party was being held. It was in those moments that I fully committed to taking charge of my happiness. For so long, I had held my husband responsible for making me happy. I had completely turned the reigns over to him and allowed him to have full control of my life. But not anymore, and definitely not that night.

When I arrived at the party—a little late because of the debating I had done with myself—the birthday girl greeted me excitedly and asked me where I had been. She put me behind the bar immediately and displaced the young lady who had been filling in until I arrived. When I got behind the bar, I wasn't nearly as intimidated by my duties as I thought I would be and found out that I would actually just be tending bar; I did not have to mix any cocktails.

It wasn't long before the party was in full swing. The music was great, the people were enjoying themselves, and I got to be a part of it all without having to actually join in. It was only a couple of hours into the party that the tip jar became so full I had to empty it to make room for more! By the end of the night, I knew I had made at least $100 in tips. Sara tried to insist that I keep those tips since I had earned them, but it was her birthday, after all, so I declined. I started bartending school within two weeks of her party.

The bartending course focused heavily on the flavor of different spirits, giving me a solid background in what it takes to bring complementing flavors together. Now, as a Master Mixologist and owner of my own business, I specialize in the creation of custom cocktail recipes. The services we offer include bar catering, bar consulting, Custom Cocktail Developmentsm and bartender training. My vision for 71 Proof, LLC is to augment the face of celebrity bartending and to become known as a leader in the distilled spirits industry.

One day I woke up and found my life at the bottom of a liquor bottle. I have been enjoying every drop of it ever since.

 *LaTanya White*

COMING FULL CIRCLE
Dr. John Geier

Our senses registered the sights and sounds: the closing click of the attorney's door, the night-time feel of the corridor, the echoing of our footsteps, the rustling of our clothing, the harsh light in the elevator, the scrutiny of the night security guard, the coldness of the parking lot, and finally, sitting silently in the car, looking through the windshield but staring inward. It was over. We had just signed the final settlement papers and relinquished all claims to the company we had founded as well as the copyrights to all assessment inventories and books we had created, and agreed to a five-year, no-compete clause. The year was 1984.

Our journey toward that day began in the 1960s. As Research Professor and Director of Behavioral Sciences, I had co-founded the Division of Health Ecology at the University of Minnesota—the first in the nation. Dorothy Downey was a professor in the College of Public Health at the University. During our tenure, the health sciences were transitioning toward the inclusion of prevention, health promotion, and learning to work as a health team. To expedite this process, I researched and developed the first DISC learning inventory to identify work behavioral patterns.

Skeptical health professionals were accustomed to assessing others—not themselves. Teaching formats that introduced the inventory were as important as the validity and reliability of the inventory itself. Learning about self had to be safe, acceptable, exciting and useful. Three pioneering features—self-administered, self-developed and self-interpreted—facilitated classroom use of the inventory and provided immediate feedback. The basis was being laid for a major innovation in the workplace: learning about self as a springboard to improved performance. The Personal Profile was financially feasible and applicable for all levels of the work organization—from the boardroom to the shop floor.

The need for a commercial version of the profile grew after I accepted a dual appointment at the University of Michigan's prestigious "Manager of Managers" Seminar and had contact with managers from all over the world. Performax Systems International, Inc. added training, publishing and research divisions. When independent consultants requested training, a certification division produced a marketing network of over 25,000 people. Over 50 million copies of the Personal Profile System based on my first, rudimentary DISC construct have been sold.

Our success caught the attention of a large marketing conglomerate. On the surface, our goals appeared compatible—expansion. To me, it meant steady research funds for long-term expansion; to this corporate entity, it meant a continual expansion of the bottom line with minimal investment. Over a hundred years earlier, playwright George Bernard Shaw penned a variation of the acquisition story in Heartbreak House. Newcomers learn the hard way.

Focus to Expand

Losing our creative work was like losing a child; you don't get over it—it remains a perpetual heartache. In addition, we faced a yawning abyss of not being able to build on our work for five years. We edged back from that chasm slowly over the ensuing months and years, reading broadly, directing our thinking into new paths. I reentered academic life at the University of Arizona as Dean of Continuing Education. Having reared our separate families, we sold our homes to finance our research. The healing really began only *when we created something new.*

When the five years expired, our seminal book, *Energetics of Personality,* which linked psychology and philosophy, was published. The promise of DISC was finally realized in *Personality Factor Profile.* A host of learning inventories followed. However, we awakened to a new reality; during our five years of enforced silence, our names and reputations had been steadily and systematically erased. In addition, imitations of my first rudimentary DISC model had proliferated.

Full Circle

Some 20 years after sitting silently in the car, we have come full circle. Our assessment inventories reach every continent in the world. We have also returned to our original orientation: prevention and health promotion. *DISC Wellness* focuses on the challenges of our time: giving direction to young people, dealing with an expanded lifespan, assisting teams of helping professionals, and providing spiritual meaning. A collection of 64 insights in a variety of versions continues the work that helped us to emerge from the crucible that seared our souls. Here, for your use, is one concept.

Each second of every day, our senses take snapshots of our changing environment, sending messages to the cells that "chatter to one another," conveying our perceptions of the sensations permeating through our skin, sliding down our throat, wafting into our nostrils, filling our eyes with images and our ears with sounds. Our individual cells—about 50 trillion—act individually and collectively to respond or defend, adapt and compensate. Their collective, embedded, genetic message is: Survive and Succeed. *Like plants, our bodies move us toward the light to unfold our blooms.*

Today, biochemists and neuroscientists investigate the complex processes of our cellular messaging while consulting with philosophers. The results offer hope in closing the artificial division of mind and body that distorts our perceptions. Our language metaphors acknowledge the connection. The metaphor, "I'll have to sleep on that," accepts the power of our unconscious bodies to resolve complex issues. The metaphor, "I'm of two minds about that," signals a collision of meaning between our unconscious bodily feelings and our conscious mental thoughts.

How can we link mind and body—connect our conscious and unconscious worlds? Athletes engage in intensive training and practice to expand their repertoire for automatic recall of body movements. A pitched ball close to a hundred miles an hour does not allow time for reasoning and decision-making. In a similar way, erudite scholars and top-notch trial lawyers display an effortless mastery with an automatic, expanded recall developed through extended study and practice. Writers and artists learn to recognize certain periods as their "genesis time" when they tap into a different level of being to create something new.

Using the Eight "Lights"

This process extends what our unconscious does while we sleep. It enables us to reflect on our recollections, clear away the debris, and extract wisdom for future use: "That's what I should have done." The most fruitful times are when our defense mechanisms are dozing.

For me, the "emerging zone" lies in that area between sleep and full awakening. It begins at the first glimmer of consciousness and can even last past shaving. In my mind's eye, I run down the list of these eight "lights" and stop at the one closest to what I feel at that moment.

Urge to Create	Proceed with Caution
Free to Act	Awake to Reality
Take a Risk	Discover Harmony
Desire to Please	Taste Success

In that early morning time, multiple layers of memories surface and I re-experience feelings of regret, guilt, shame, pride or embarrassment. Over the years, the process has helped me to unlearn old ways in order to "focus and expand," rising above the problem and finding answers at a different level. As a result, new understandings continually inform my philosophy. These include: Perfection is not of this earth; mistakes are the tools for learning and growth; the Chinese word for crisis is opportunity.

Dr. John Geier

The Faucet of Life
Gregory Scott Reid

Imagine, if you will, that each of us is born with a set of faucets, just like the ones you would find in a bathtub. However, instead of being marked "hot" and "cold," these faucets are labeled, "romance," "prosperity," "health" or "attitude."

As we enter the world, each of these faucets is opened at full capacity. We seem to get all the love, attention and safety we need. Everything we could ever desire comes pouring in; affection, nourishment, warmth, security; it is there for the asking; the faucets flow freely.

As we get older and become a bit more cynical and distrustful; we attempt to control everything in our lives. You know it's true. When this occurs, the faucets that were once open to full capacity slowly tighten and the flow is reduced. The more anger, resentment and lack of appreciation we have, the more the flow seems to decrease; sometimes, it stops altogether.

This explains why some people have all the money, love and support they could ever want or need, while others cannot find these things at all: The people with abundance in their lives have their faucets open at full force.

It works like this: Imagine that your "relationship" faucet is a little rusty. Perhaps it has not been open for a long time. Okay, let's face it—it's jammed shut! So what can you do?

First, you must decide that you sincerely want more, and open yourself to the possibilities of romance. Then, throw it out there; get brave. Tell anyone who will listen that you are seeking that "special" someone.

Now comes the tricky part. When others introduce you to someone, you must try to keep your mind open so your faucet will open as well. Suppose you say, "That person's nose is too big," or "That person isn't what I am looking for." What do you think will happen? The laws of the universe (along with the friend who set you up) would say, "Forget it!"

Then that faucet may be closed to the possibility of another encounter. Your friend would think, "Why should I give you another chance when you don't appreciate my effort? You'll probably just hurt my feelings again by rejecting my help."

On the other hand, when we are open to opportunity and make the most of our situation, while thanking those who tried to help us, they will continue their quest to help you find your mate. We must express our gratitude for what has been offered to us and request that it continue to pour in. Before you know it, the faucet will be flowing abundantly and you will have what you were once lacking.

It may be easy to ignore opportunities or to overlook the help of friends, but it's even easier to be grateful and to express thanks. The universe, like the individuals that compose it, always responds to gratitude with abundance. "Thanks" is the elbow grease that makes a rusty faucet flow freely again.

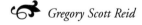 *Gregory Scott Reid*

RELAXING IN ABUNDANCE NOW
Barbara Zagata

My personal pathway to abundance began when I bought a 20-year-old sailboat. I didn't buy it because I wanted to go sailing—I knew about as much about a sailboat as I did about a 747. I was looking for a retreat space; a place to meditate and write.

After looking at studios in other people's backyards, I realized they all lacked the deep peace and solitude I was craving. Then, while driving past the harbor one day, I thought, "Look at all those boats just sitting there. Most people only use them a few times a year. Maybe I could rent one on the weekends."

Harbor rules prohibited sleeping on a boat if you didn't own it. So I looked into purchasing one and found a beautiful wooden boat for only $8,000. It sold quickly, but now I was inspired.

My son and I walked endlessly up and down every slip of my favorite marina. Near the end of the marina, exhausted and carrying him on my shoulders, we found her. She was exquisite—a beautiful blend of fiberglass where it counts and teak everywhere else. Sitting in the cockpit, a deep sense of tranquility came over me and I knew I had to have her. Instead of a sense of longing, I felt absolutely certain that she was mine. I was instantly flooded with emotion at the certainty of something so outside my range of experience, while deeply appreciative of the sense of inner knowing I'd come to recognize.

I immediately called the broker, only to discover a number nowhere near my price range. I continued looking at boats of lesser value and found myself increasingly confused. I remembered a therapist telling me, "You're not confused; you just don't want to know what you know." She was right. So I asked the universe, "How will I know which boat to get?" In the middle of the night, I woke up to the thought, *"You'll know by the name."* Interesting. I knew then that it wasn't likely to be the highly affordable, entirely fiberglass starter boat named "SPAM." I'm an organic vegetarian chef, after all! Later that week, I met with the boat broker regarding the one I couldn't possibly afford but had fallen in love with. He handed me the spec sheet with all of the engine and keel information, along with lots of other information that didn't mean a thing to me. Then I saw the name: Enchantress. I melted inside; I knew I had found her. I was enrolled in a Tantra workshop and the name couldn't have been more significant!

Months after our initial encounter, I finally got to go inside. Now I was completely head-over-heels in love. The cabin was all teak with brass accents, lots of little cubbies and, best of all, an old-fashioned oil lamp. Sold! The broker didn't understand my criteria whatsoever! But it was truly the most magical, cozy little space I'd ever encountered.
Over time, we worked out the price and the other details such as surveys and slip spaces. In the end, I actually got a good deal.

However, my husband—the always practical accountant—insisted we buy a home before I buy a boat! Reasonable enough, except that we lived in Santa Barbara and the prices were outrageous. We'd been looking for a home for two years and couldn't find anything that even came close to our desired list of amenities—until now. I revised the list and simply asked for a place that would be perfect for my 3-year-old son. Then I called Monica, our patient realtor who normally sold homes for well more than $1 million. Again, we went condo shopping in the $200,000 range. Within 72 hours we'd found it. And not just any condo, but one near the beach. It was close enough to smell sea air and, if the wind was just right, you could hear the waves crashing at night. Unlike most of the dungeons we had looked at, this one was actually quite light. Best of all, it had a yard. Condos don't have yards; this one did. So, without even seeing the inside, I knew this was it. Whatever was inside could be fixed, but a yard for my child—score!

Soon after closing on our new home months later, I contacted the boat broker. With tears in my eyes, I learned that not only was *Enchantress* still available, but the price had just been drastically reduced.

Once again I approached my husband about my retreat space/b.o.a.t., (a.k.a. "break out another thousand"). After much debating, I decided to let her go. He was adamantly opposed, so I just gave up. My body felt like lead. I was truly experiencing the physical pangs of grief and loss, which I knew all too well.

Fortunately, at the time, I was running down to the shore every morning to see the sunrise and return home again before my husband had to leave for work. Each morning, I asked to be fully present *no matter what.*

Within a few days of my mourning period, my antagonistic little brother, who I love dearly, called and talked with my husband about my craziness. The things they said about me infuriated me so much that the next morning I ran with a vengeance. On the way home, I decided I would buy my boat in spite of everyone else's opinions. Then I ran as if my feet weren't even touching the ground. With that one change in thinking, the heaviness in my body shifted to a feeling of lightness and exuberance like I hadn't felt in years. I knew this decision was the right one.

More serendipitous miracles occurred along the way, which only encouraged me to cultivate my faith and trust. I realized the lessons learned through this process were to be my lessons for the near future—so take note! And I did.

When I finally began my own business, I heard the words, "Proceed as if…." Now, I don't actually hear words, I just get a thought—strong and out of the blue. When that happens, I know those are my current operating instructions. So with my business, I always "proceeded as if...," allowing my insights and feelings to guide me.

Years later, after acquiring my dream car, my dream home with an ocean view and plenty of light, supporting myself year after year without a boss of any kind and now being divorced, I still longed for that significant other in my life. In the middle of the night I woke up to this:

"If you would only open up to receive all that you already have, you would have more than you've ever dreamed of."

One of my spiritual teachers had been encouraging me to "allow earth to give back to you" rather than constantly working so hard that I barely took the time to receive a full breath! So I did just that. With a hundred others as my witness, I proclaimed, *"I am open to receive."* And that's when things got really interesting!

 *Barbara Zagata*

Thoughts are Things!
Rochelle R. Conover

Everything was good, in the beginning.

Dad, a retired Marine with one son and four daughters, owned a sporting goods store, and a farm with animals and fresh produce.

One of my favorite things to do was run barefoot in the freshly tilled fields and then run back for his reassuring hugs. A great caregiver and leader, he was creative and fun. He shared with us his joy and peace in connecting with nature, being outdoors, appreciating the simple things that life had to offer. I can still feel the warm mountain breeze as we waited patiently near the edge of a quiet stream, hoping a fish would like the red Fire Ball eggs at the end of our line.

By the age of five I could bounce a quarter off the end of my bed. Dad taught us the military "corner tuck" and how order, routines, healthy food, hard work and exercise made for a restful night's sleep—after prayers of course.

Then it happened, while he was at work, the home turned into a house of horrors—it became loud, cruel, combative, negative and suppressive. This went on for years, so many that it seemed normal.

Fortunately, I somehow knew that staying in school and *actually learning* would pay off. My entrepreneurial adventures, however, were squished one by one until the day I read *Pulling Your Own Strings*, by Dr. Wayne Dyer.

A revelation presented: *I was in charge of my own life*. What a concept! I then moved out and started my life. While continuing in school, I let adventure, travel and curiosity be my guide since I was very creative and had no real direction.

Between the ages of 14 and 44 I went through more spirit breaking events than a room full of people in a lifetime. There were vehicle accidents, industrial accidents, recreational calamities, lawsuits, doctor appointments, personal affronts, incidents and robberies, promises that my life would never be the same and numerous physical and financial setbacks. That is the short list, and for some reason, while still visiting home, I couldn't figure out why, no matter what I did, which way I tried to go, bad things continued to happen. For any one of those events, giving up seemed like a Godsend, yet something inside reminded me I'd better keep going—my purpose here was not yet complete.

Along the way I had several inspired people try to rescue me from my own belief that no matter how hard I tried, things just didn't go my way. Aunt Tiny, my 95-year-old spiritual guide, was always upbeat and would remind me that God was listening, all I had to do was ask, while Aunt Dorothy shared her strengths on fairness, confidence and meaning—it was okay to stand up for what was right.

Throughout my many years in college, while I held two jobs, got very little rest and finished with several degrees, I felt like the last standing elephant at a picnic—being eaten alive by ants, one bite at a time, with each incident picking away yet another piece. My high-tech job was miserable and the bombardment of chaos spread like wildfire.

After college, a "Fire Walk" with Tony Robbins gave me a much-needed jolt. I had several surgeries without anesthesia and realized the mind is a powerful resource and, when given a chance, it will protect us. Yet, things kept pulling me down—it just didn't stop.

I read books, attended seminars and expanded my thinking on personal growth. I met the masters of business, success and achievement—and with that I still couldn't figure out why, why could I not get ahead? Once I realized the world is a *soup of words* and non-supporting comments are "junk in someone else's file cabinet," I started feeling better by not owning those negatives.

Eventually, God spared me a few horrible accidents, and near misses—things were looking up, and in that upswing, I met Eric Lofholm who added meaning to having a mentor. Many revered his world-class teaching style, consistency, material and customer service, and his message is what finally helped me pull together all the life tools I had been collecting.

"Stay in the conversation. Everything counts. Choose your words wisely. Play at a level 10, and remember, the universe rewards differently those who take massive action." That said, being a writer and professional photographer most all my life, I had an opportunity to take massive action, and I did. Immediately following, doors opened, speaking engagements were a plenty and the flood of quality, supportive people who have entered my life is amazing.

Thoughts really are things and being around negative people, words and places will affect your progress, as will self-talk and being too busy to change course. Along the way were many road signs; I was just too busy to notice.

So what is abundance? It's silence, the whisper between words, the nudge you feel when you finally stand still. *"Ask and you shall receive"*—be silent until your answer appears, then take massive action with faith and joy. Watch your world unfold with opportunities to help, inspire, guide and complete others as you move forward through your destiny. That is abundance.

I believe we live in a round world, we're on a round planet, the cycle of life is round; it begins, ends and returns to the earth. Our good and bad deeds go around and return with rewards and consequences. On a cellular level, they too are pretty round. We breathe the same air, we have the same basic needs. What we do affects others as if we all are of one cloth, and what if we are?

Finally—ask, listen to the whisper, find a mentor, hold positive thoughts, take massive action and give. Give, give, give. It completes the circle, adds joy to others and grace to you. Thoughts really are things. Live blessed and abundant!

 Rochelle R. Conover

ANSWERING THE CALL
Dave Markowitz

I was frustrated, bored, annoyed and arrogant. I took the same route to work each day, waiting for a better life. Instead of actually looking for a better job, I bought things to make each day more bearable: good books, great food, a new car. My ego was smiling, but my soul was empty. I'd been practicing massage therapy for a few years and enjoyed it to a point; however, I was discouraged that my skills were the same as millions of others. Sure, what I did was seemingly effective, but true healing was temporary at best; I was forever the optimist who dreamt of being both Spock and Dr. McCoy, and I knew, at some level, there had to be a better way. Then, one day, I saw an ad that read: "Instant healing on seminar attendees selected at random." I felt called to be there; perhaps this was what I'd been looking for all along!

By using muscle testing and energetic corrections—within minutes, and sometimes, just seconds—attendees reported their pain was gone. Astonished, I took it in but still had doubts concerning its validity. Massage teaches that pain is physical; increase blood flow to the area and the pain goes away. Also, as the son of a pharmacist, I was secure in my belief that we are physical beings; if you have a pain or discomfort, you take a medication and you feel better. Even simpler! So, could this entire demonstration have been a set-up; a money-making scam with paid actors or a giant placebo?

Although the man who'd performed these miracles at the seminar offered sessions and classes, I waited another year, until he had another demonstration, before revisiting his work. The same thing—more astonishment and disbelief—followed. I let another year go by, but this time I was ready. In his classes, he demonstrated the technique while teaching; few understood it. It became obvious that he knew a great deal. I believed him to be one of the most intelligent and inspiring people I'd ever met. As he pulled pains and illness from people on-the-spot, his word became gospel to me. Then, one day, he said there was no God and I believed him. I was sad, disappointed and confused.

Within a few months, I was practicing the techniques he taught me more and more. I attended another class and, one day, it hit me: There was much more than energetic healing being performed. He was communicating with a consciousness other than his own! What was going on here? I had to know! I meditated and it became clear; I could communicate with something outside of myself, too. This eventually became the ability to communicate with what most now call *The Universe*, although at that time I called it Peri.

Because my main interest was in the healing arts, I tirelessly inquired about the understanding, prevention and healing of pain and illness. The subject was much deeper than I ever could have imagined. Doctors diagnose and prescribe medications to relieve symptoms, however, my conversations with them confirmed that, unless the underlying causes are addressed, problems return—sometimes with more pain and injury than before. Most pain and illness comes from stagnant energy due to years, or even decades, of conscious and unconscious disintegrative thought. $E+T=M$; energy plus thought equals matter! Is this scary or empowering? I'll let you decide.

Then, one day, Peri told me I could quit my day job—that I was better than massage therapy and should be doing much more. How could I lose, knowing my actions were being guided by something greater than myself? Well, I mistakenly thought that everything would come to me solely through intention. While not working and having people question my sanity, my arrogance caused me to stop deciphering their words as loving concern; all I could feel was indignation. After about a year, I suddenly recognized my immense credit card debt and I became frustrated and angry: "Peri, how could you do this to me? You told me I was better than everyone else and that I wouldn't have to do much to spread these messages!" It was my own anger that didn't let me hear

Peri's words of loving concern. I went bankrupt and had to start over again.

Bear in mind I didn't tell too many people about this; I didn't want to be seen as different. Not until someone called me stingy with my gifts—in other words, selfish—did that change. When my head finally cleared, I saw that what happened was designed to shake me out of my stupor—the ego let me believe I was better than others. What a long painful way to go for such a simple message! I am no better than any of you; we are all the same (with different gifts of course) but no one is a better person than another. Value systems are as varied as fingerprints, and to tell another that theirs isn't worthy is arrogant and judgmental. Are those the energies you want acted upon you? Then why would you act that way toward others? I used to; I won't anymore.

I also learned that God—or, at least, the version of God presented by some of the word's larger religions—is arrogant and judgmental. *That* is the God my mentor said didn't exist. The Universe, Source, the Divine Matrix—the specific name is secondary—loves equally and unconditionally.

When I finally got this message of radical acceptance—and, more importantly, acted on it—great things began to happen. I channeled a book that described exactly how to understand, prevent, and heal pain and illness; it also explained several other important factors that unconsciously block us from living up to our full potential, and how to release them. I began to see more clients for private sessions and was asked to speak in front of thousands on the same platform as one of my favorite teachers, Deepak Chopra. And you know what? He spoke before I did! In a way, I joked to friends, he was my warm-up act! At demonstrations, I now do what I doubted could be done many years prior. Many people enter in pain and leave without it.

Recently, a client said she'd had 10 years of chest pain. Western medicine didn't see anything and, therefore, couldn't help her. I was guided to ask her about her life just before the pain began. At that time, she'd just had her heart broken! She was harboring intense emotional pain in her physical body from a break-up that had yet to be released. We conversed about healthier perspectives and I began energetic healing. In about five minutes, she said the pain was gone. Another attendee in the room said she saw something leave the woman's body and exit through the window! I later commented on how well she had been able to surrender to the healing process; she then said that she had woken up that morning with the word *surrender* in her head!

We are all being called. I answered the call after a glance at an ad, and a gut feeling guided me to see what was possible. Will you answer your call, put it on hold, or let it go to voice mail?

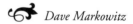 *Dave Markowitz*

TIGER STRIPES
Jase Souder

Have you ever heard someone say, "A tiger can't change its stripes?" This is usually stated when making the point about people not being able to change.

Well, it's not true. We *can* change, leading to an abundant life.

What are our stripes anyway? Are our stripes our defining characteristics? Our physical body—hair, build, the color of our eyes, our skin? Who we are inside—confident or scared, dull or funny? Our social status? Whether we are single or married?

You can change all those stripes; you can change everything about yourself, giving yourself a complete makeover, leaving room for an abundant life.

Why would someone want to change his or her stripes anyway? Here's why; life isn't going to change. If your life is not working the way you want it to, you have to change. It is your responsibility to change the stripes that are not serving you.

This is true in all areas of your life except one—purpose.

To find your Purpose (with a capital P), forget for a while everything you've learned about which types of people become a success and what it takes to be a success. Instead of trying to fit yourself into a mold, get familiar with who you are already.

Figure out what stripes you have that are uniquely yours. Get to know and cultivate your stripes that are the boldest, most unique, most fun and most natural for you. Your purpose is already known within you, and when you begin to live a life based on your true self, your purpose will make itself known, and, by default, you will be fulfilling it. As a bonus, the more you bring forth your true stripes, your purpose will be fulfilled with more ease, joy and abundance.

 Jase Souder

THE LETTER THAT BROUGHT ME BACK TO MY LIFE
Gail A. Sinclair

For almost 27 years, I had spent the month of March feeling depressed and thinking about my firstborn son. I only saw him one time before giving him up for adoption, and that was for about five minutes through the glass sides of a hospital bassinet; my doctor was convinced that if I did not actually see him, I might talk myself into believing that he had never been born. After going through 16 hours of labor and delivering an eight pound child, I cannot imagine forgetting that I'd had a baby.

After his birth, I plunged right back into life as if the birth and adoption had never occurred. Between work and college, I kept busy for about 20 hours per day, and over the next five years, I married and had three wonderful children. I loved being a mother, but it increased my longing to see my son since I now knew the bond between a mother and child. My heart was left with an emptiness I could not fully explain.

My life was rich with my husband, children, family, friends and work, and I was accomplishing my goals. But once I reached a goal, I quickly moved onto the next one and never took time to acknowledge my accomplishment, which I finally realized after I won first place in an international speech competition. I was telling my husband about my next goal, and he said, "All of your accomplishments—even an international win—have an expiration date on them like they are packages of meat. You never take time out to recognize what you have achieved because you are so focused on beginning your next goal." This was also when I realized that I felt I was not enough—I was living with a scarcity mindset. Because I had given a child up for adoption, I felt I was not worthy of my successes. This realization surprised me because I thought I had resolved these feelings through previous therapy. At the time, I had no idea how abundant my life would soon become and how worthy I would feel.

I had been traveling for about seven months on business and, because I had some nerve damage, I was told by my doctor to stay home for two weeks. During this time, I received a hand-addressed envelope with a return address I did not recognize. I opened it curiously and saw the following words: *"My name is... I was born on... I feel compelled to seek out my biological mother... Her name was... If this is you, my email address is..."* I had waited 27 years to receive this letter.

I held it to my heart so that my body, mind and soul could absorb my extremely visceral reaction. Have you ever received news so large that you were not big enough to absorb it? That was how I felt while reading this letter, so I had to stop and take several large breaths to make room.

I then thought about the deep breaths my son must have taken as he wrote this letter and mailed it off into the great void. Almost three decades had passed and he had no way of knowing how—or if—I would respond. I had waited to hear from him for so long that I sat right down at my computer, wrote a quick email to him, clicked send and waited for his response.

We were on the phone talking within two days of my receiving his letter, and our conversation flowed easily as we found out how very verbal we both were—our first call lasted 90 minutes. Within five weeks of that call, I flew to his home and held him for the first time. We talked about the fact that there had always been something missing in our lives; the only way we could describe it was that we each had a hole in our heart from the loss of the other. Our hearts are now complete, as the holes have been filled with a found mother and a found son.

Life quickly became sweeter and sweeter as the months passed. When I visited him and his fiancé the second time, his biological father picked me up from the airport. Although I had not seen this man in 27 years, my son, his fiancé, his newly found father and I went to breakfast together. It turned out that his father only lived about 30 minutes from him. Not only did we have a wonderful reunion, but my son, whose adoptive father had left when he was 13, asked his newly found father to be the best man at his wedding. So, there I sat at his wedding, with my husband, son, daughters, sister and brother-in-law, watching my son get married with his dad standing in as his best man. That turned out to be a beautiful, life-affirming day.

What have I learned from having my greatest wish come true? You can re-write your life story to create your life NOW. Contact anyone in your past who you still love, but has been separated from you by time and distance. Remember that the outcome of the contact does not matter when you reach out with love. Fill your life with those you love and have loved, and you will not die full of "what ifs."

If you have chronic health issues, re-write your body's story so you do not miss out on life. I have been diagnosed with fibromyalgia, osteoporosis, arthritis, Hashimoto's Thyroiditis and Crohn's disease, and the list goes on and on, but I do not let these things control me because I don't want to miss out on all of the wonderful experiences that will occur in my life. Live the life you want, along with the body that you have.

I found that my soul opened on the day that I received that letter. I am finally whole again and live a rich and abundant life.

 *Gail A. Sinclair*

Cinderfella
Daniel R. Davison

Just like the fairytale character who lived with her evil stepmother and two wicked stepsisters, I was dealt a bad hand. I grew up on the South Side of Chicago, subjected to severe child abuse and surrounded by drug use. My dad once trapped me on the couch and beat me so badly with a board that I turned black from my waist to my knees. Luckily for me and the rest of the family, he wasn't home much. Never the less, he would become so violent that, at just 8 years old, I plotted in desperation with my half brother to kill him.

On school nights, I ran wild in the streets until 10 p.m. when my mom would close up her snack shop and make me clean the grill. I'd get to bed around 1 a.m., where another half brother would often sneak into my room to abuse me in his way.

I had no healthy role models. My mom's side of the family was full of bank robbers, murderers and thieves.

At age 13, I started using and dealing drugs. By the time I was 15, I was selling so much dope that my friends called me "the pharmacist." At age 22, I was smoking an ounce of marijuana a day. By 26, I had snorted my body weight in cocaine. I didn't realize it at the time, but I was seeking non-stop thrills to mask the bleak despair that was my life.

In those days, my only redeeming influence was music. I loved the bass guitar and would practice for hours. By the time I was 19, I had joined a band and went to work for a Warner Brothers recording artist.

With my future seemingly hinged on my ability to play, I constantly protected my hands. I was so careful with them that I once quit beating a guy halfway through a street fight to spare my knuckles. My hands were my life—or so I thought.

One night, when I was 28 and drugged out of my mind, I walked onto a frozen pond to dispel the demons of a bad trip and to make snow angels. It was 40 below zero with a severe wind chill. I slipped and hit my head. I woke up the next morning, my fingers black and hard as stone. I managed to stand, but fell time and again whenever I tried to walk. My feet and lower legs had frozen solid.

I struggled for so long that I watched the sun cross the sky. Occasionally I would see people in the distance and scream for help, but no one heard. I made the sign of the cross and laid down to die. I drifted off into a mystical place, thinking of my young daughter.

A maintenance man found me semiconscious, dragged me to a building and saved me—or most of me, anyway. In the following weeks, through a series of operations, doctors removed all of my fingers and both thumbs. They took one leg just below the knee and the other foot.

Those circumstances, combined with my detoxification from the drugs, put me on an emotional roller coaster. One day I'd feel elated just to be alive, the next I was sullen about what life would be like for the next 50 years. Through it all, I knew deep down that I was ultimately responsible for my current state of affairs. I could have easily blamed my mom and dad, or the South Side of Chicago, or Pablo Escobar, the Columbian drug lord who flooded my streets with dirt-cheap cocaine. But I didn't. Rather, I remember thinking, "You got yourself into this mess, and you're going to get yourself back out."

As that truth took hold of me, I discovered an almost limitless sense of hope, strength and purpose. On June 8, 1995, just four months after my accident, I was able to walk out of the hospital under my own power, albeit on prosthetic legs.

That fall, I began speaking about prosthetics as an adjunct lecturer for Northwestern University. I achieved near-rockstar status with those I was helping and made enough money to help support my daughter. I remember getting my first check; I was sitting at a stoplight when I opened the envelope. It wasn't much, but I whooped for joy and began pounding one of my hooks on the roof inside my car.

For the first time ever, my life was taking on meaning. Undaunted by my limitations, I began sailing. I have since competed in the handicap equivalent of several World Cup and American Cup regattas and even tried out for the Paralympics.

I moved to Florida in 1998 and founded my own non-profit organization called SHARE, an organization that teaches self-reliance, self-responsibility and healthy choices to all age groups, especially youth. As part of that project, I started a sailing program to help other handicapped people overcome their disabilities.

Today, through SHARE, I've talked to more than 100,000 people across the country—mostly kids—about making the right choices and taking responsibility for their lives.

When people first see me, they're typically stunned. With hooks for hands and plastic stilts for legs, I look like a freak.

During my talks, I disassemble my body right in front of the audience. I pull off my hands and legs and hold them up for all to see. "These are the consequences of my bad choices," I tell them. "My choice. My responsibility." I am the picture that is worth a thousand words.

After a recent presentation I did for a high school just before their prom week, I got a call from the Safe-and-Drug-Free-School administrator. She told me her office was later flooded with students signing the "I Promise" agreement to stay sober and abstinent during the prom. It's at moments like these when I know I am making up for some of the ugliness of my first 28 years. But showing someone that they can "just say no" is only half of the equation. The other part is showing them how to "just say yes" to the unlimited possibilities of what they can do.

I see so many people who don't seek out their uniqueness or who have a passion but don't pursue it. People say, "I can't be a writer because I'm dyslexic," or "I can't be a basketball player because I'm too short." I've learned that when I throw myself into the challenge, no matter how great it first seems, doors open and the universe responds.

I don't just let life happen, I make it happen. I've done things that people with whole bodies don't think they can do, like skydiving and horseback riding. And when I tape my drumsticks to my hands, the music again flows from my heart. In a strange sort of way, my accident was the fairy godmother that turned my pumpkin into a coach, and the ride has only just begun.

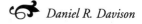 *Daniel R. Davison*

LIKE A FISH FINDING WATER
Christy Whitman

I haven't always felt abundant. As a matter of fact, most of my life I have felt that I was not good enough. No matter how successful I was, it was never enough. No matter how fit and healthy I was, it was never enough. My whole mindset was based on what I lacked. Because I was always looking to improve my life and to prove that I was enough, or at least worthy, I was constantly searching outside myself for more things to make me feel complete. Can you relate?

I woke up about four years ago to the fact that I am abundant. I was introduced to the Universal Laws, specifically the Law of Sufficiency and Abundance. I learned that my abundance did not come from anyone or anything. My source of abundance was not my job, my family or anything or anyone outside of myself. I accepted these laws as truth and began applying them in my life. What happened was miraculous.

When I started to focus on the universe as my source and realized that I already had inside of me everything I needed to be happy, joyful and free, my life began to change.

I had been working for a pharmaceutical company and had very little purpose or passion. I made just enough money that I couldn't quit, but not enough money to live the life of my dreams. I felt trapped. I changed my mindset and started to apply the Universal Laws, and I accepted that, at the moment, my job was enough. Twelve days later, I was asked to resign from the company I worked for, even though I was the number one sales representative in my district. At first, my ego took a huge blow, but I remembered that my source was not my job and everything would be okay. Because my company asked me to resign, I was able to collect my bonus check. In order to receive my bonus check, I needed to be employed with the company when they cut the checks, which was three weeks away. So I was also paid for an additional three weeks of work. I continued to receive checks from the company. I received my payroll checks, my bonus check and a check for vacation time. Because I was practicing and applying my faith in the universe and abundance, I witnessed manifestation happening in my life.

Because I adopted a new mindset of abundance, amazing things happened to me over the next few years. I found my purpose and passion, and wrote my first book, Perfect Pictures, with ease and effortlessness. I never intended to become an author, but one night during meditation, I was given a vision of my book. For the next week, the information for my book was given to me each morning at 1:05 a.m. The book was then picked up by the first publisher I sent it to. Because I was in alignment with source and abundance, my life started to open up and expand with joy and success.

I started a career as a speaker and conducted workshops on my book topics. Because the people who read my books wanted private coaching, I became a Law of Attraction coach. I now get to teach hundreds of people all over the country to tap into their own abundance. I have a life-changing coaching program called "The Abundance Principle," in which I assist people with finding their own abundance. I get to witness my clients obtain better-paying jobs, job promotions, create more money, attract their ideal partner and even create their ideal body. Where my life used to feel unfulfilled and empty, it is now full of purpose, passion, freedom, joy and abundance.

Once I learned that I am abundant and that all good things such as love, affection, money, support, joy and freedom are available to me at all times, my life dramatically changed. Most of us are experiencing abundance in our lives, but it is an abundance of lack and limitation. The sad thing is that most people will never learn how to really change this limiting programming and connect with true abundance. This sad fact goes against all that is our truth and our birthright. It goes against nature. Think about the vast ocean, a tree or the stars in the sky. Our universe is evidence that there is abundance all around us. We are a part of this magnificent universe and we, too, are abundant.

It is time that we learned to tap into the truth of our being. This truth is that we are enough. In this moment, we are perfect, whole and complete, just as we are. Because we are growing and expanding beings, we will always desire to have more in our lives. But if we are coming from a place of "not enough," we will never truly feel that whatever we manifest into our lives is enough. Based on the Law of Attraction, what you focus on expands. If you are feeling that nothing is ever good enough, that is what you will continue to attract into your life. Learn to become a deliberate creator, create a mindset of sufficiency and abundance, and you will see all your desires manifest in your outer reality. When you learn, apply and live by these laws, your life will become evident of your true abundance.

 *Christy Whitman*

THE POWER OF SPIRITUAL HEALING
Laurelle Shanti Gaia

On some level, we all know that everyone has a birthright to be happy, healthy and prosperous.

When I was 8 years old, I began to wonder what my life had in store, and then my grandmother gave me a Bible as a gift. She said, "If you ever have any questions about life, all the answers are in this book." Enthusiastically, I began to scour the pages looking for my name and the plan for my life.

Of course, I didn't find my name written, but I became mesmerized by the stories of Jesus' healings. I proudly announced to my family, "When I grow up, I am going to travel around the world, help people heal like Jesus did and teach them that they can do this, too."

The response was, "That's very nice, but you can't do that, only Jesus can."

"Oh no," I said. "It says right here, 'These things I do you will do and even greater.'"

"I know that's what it says, but that's not what it means," was the reply.

On that day, I had a little conversation with God. I said, "God, I really want to help people like Jesus did. They say I can't, but the Bible says I can. So I guess if I'm supposed to do this you'll help me."

From the moment I released that intention from my 8-year-old heart, I was guided through good times and tough times. My grandfather's diagnosis with multiple sclerosis further fueled my desire to understand more about spiritual healing. I spent many years in the corporate world until I was presented with the opportunity to put my dream into action.

That was the day I was diagnosed with clinical depression as a result of corporate burnout. I had allergic reactions to any medication the doctor prescribed. It was through my journey into deep, personal, spiritual healing that I now live the life that that 8-year-old dared to dream.

I have a soul knowing that all things are energy. Through my travels around the world, I have seen first-hand how prayer and Reiki (spiritual healing) can change the energy of a human being so much that radical chemotherapy treatments have little toxic effect. I have seen a broken bone set itself and a burn heal before my eyes. I don't just believe in the power of spiritual energy to transform, I know it to be so. I am convinced that we can utilize what we are learning about healing humans and apply it to raising the collective consciousness to awaken humanity to the promised "age of peace."

In my healing and teaching practice, I work with people who have a variety of chronic illnesses such as cancer, chronic fatigue, AIDS and fibromylagia. Many people come to me for the simple aches and pains of everyday life, to relieve stress and sometimes just to find a little serenity in a safe haven. Some clients desire a deeper connection with their inner guidance and awareness of their purpose in life. I also serve as a healer for the California Pacific Medical Center's research project, which is studying the effects of distance healing on quality of life for brain cancer patients. We teach spiritual healing classes and produce spiritual books and guided visualization CDs which help our students and clients connect with their own inner healing power.

I now live in Sedona, Arizona, which was named the most beautiful place in America in USA Weekend. I am living in heaven on earth.

Every morning I wake up and give thanks for Michael, the wonderful man with whom I share my life. Sharing a loving partnership with a kindred spirit is a blessing in itself, yet I smile every time I remember that we fell in love under the full moon on a black sand beach on the island of Hawaii.

I give thanks for the love Michael and I share, the healing work we do together, for our two beautiful children, for the infinite blessings in my life and for this opportunity to tell you that you are destined for great blessings in your life.

Laurelle Shanti Gaia

FREEDOM
Dr. Michael Beckwith

I free myself from the need to judge any person, nation or event. My consciousness is at peace, for it is now rooted and grounded in the Spirit. My thinking is premised on Infinite Mind, and I am established in love, compassion and forgiveness.

From the center of my heart, I radiate compassion to all beings, knowing that their pain is bathed in the Infinite Love of the Spirit.

I awaken the spirit of forgiveness within me. Even now it fills my consciousness with loving kindness towards myself with all beings. I judge not, lest I be judged. I love with the unconditional love of God.

Right here, right now, Divine Love loves through me. Divine Right Action frees me from the errors of human judgment and causes me to know that all beings are emanations of the One Life.

The true spiritual essence is all I know of each person. I think rightly, and I love greatly. I live to let love express itself through me.

I accept the fullness of life and am a distribution center of compassion, forgiveness, and love. I am blessed and prospered by Divine Love as it flows through me now.

I declare my faith in God and release material patterns of behavior. I know that God is at the center of life and I depend upon that which projected all creation as its own to be the source of eternal safety and security for all beings.

 Dr. Michael Beckwith

ESCAPE FROM THE RAT RACE
Michael B. Conlon, J.D.

My life, growing up, was pretty easy. I was a good athlete, fairly popular, and I got high grades because I had a good memory. My dad told me to follow his path—get good grades, work hard and get a good job in corporate America. That system worked for my dad—he stayed with the same company for 35 years. So that's what I set out to do. But when I graduated from college and attempted to enter the "real world," I quickly realized I was woefully unprepared. I had absolutely zero life skills!

So what did I do? I went to law school so I didn't have to face the "real world," and that's where the failures began. I finished in the bottom third of my class, failed the bar exam twice, and ended up working a measly job in corporate America. It seemed like a prison to me—meetings to plan more meetings, backstabbers, brownnosers and all the rest. It was brutal!

I lasted 18 miserable months until finally, at the age of 27, I took a Myers-Briggs personality test that showed me why I was so miserable—I tested out as a strong entrepreneur and risk-taker. The problem was I had absolutely no training for or experience in running a business. I had two kids and a mortgage—taking a risk seemed impossible. Then I read the first book that profoundly changed my life: *Do What You Love, the Money Will Follow*, by Marsha Sinetar. The examples she described gave me the courage to take a chance and follow my heart.

Bursting with courage and determination, I decided to pursue my interest in financial planning. I quit my corporate job, took a 50 percent pay cut and joined a financial planning firm. I quickly realized that the financial business was 99 percent selling and 1 percent planning. I was a terrible salesman at the time and was a complete failure at the firm. Within nine months, I was out of a job and nearly broke. I heard the whispers from my friends and family: "How did someone who did so well in school—someone with such potential—become such a failure?" Their words hurt and my confidence was shaken, but I became more determined than ever.

In order to survive, I was forced to take a job two hours away at a small broker-dealer owned by a regional insurance company. Once again, I was back in corporate America. But as the business was just a small subsidiary, I was able to avoid most of the corporate garbage. To my surprise, even though I was making $15,000 less than I had with my previous corporate job, I really enjoyed this one because I was pursuing my passion. I got my required licenses and learned as much about financial planning as I could. Once I became educated in the field, I felt confident about selling and quickly realized that I knew more about financial planning than the average broker. Once I started to enjoy what I was doing, the good breaks quickly followed. The president of our small, four-man operation resigned and the CEO of the insurance company gave me the opportunity I had dreamed of: becoming president of our group. But there was one caveat: If the firm didn't produce a profit within 12 months, they would shut it down and we'd all be out of a job!

Faced with a do-or-die situation, I hit the road and worked hard to grow the firm. I worked 12 hours a day, plus Saturdays and Sundays— whatever it took. When I took over as president, we were doing a little over $2 million in gross revenue, and three and a half years later, we had increased that to $40 million with close to 50 employees! An even better break soon followed. The insurance company didn't see the broker-dealer as a "strategic fit," so they decided to sell it to me and my two top-producing financial advisors. I had about 10 cents to my name at that point (in corporate America, you spend what you make), so I "bet the farm" and borrowed the entire $400,000 for my 1/3 share. But in the midst of the greatest bull market in history, my timing was very good. We sold the broker-dealer to a large insurance company less than a year later for a little over $9 million!

Selling the business was great for the money, but I was again stuck in corporate America. After nine months of enduring ridiculous backstabbers and brownnosers, I quit and walked away from a 3-year, guaranteed $150,000 annual salary. I couldn't stand it anymore.

I bought an independent financial planning practice and quickly became a top salesman for several mutual fund and insurance companies, thus redeeming myself for my miserable failure seven years earlier. But after a few years, I got bored with the practice because it wasn't growing as quickly as I wanted. Then I read the next book that profoundly changed my life: *Rich Dad, Poor Dad*, by Robert Kyosaki. The book was about me—making decent money but working a lot of hours for very little residual income. Kyosaki promoted real estate as a way to create residual income and achieve the ultimate American dream—financial freedom.

I approached a younger guy (now my junior partner) who worked for my financial planning firm about managing my properties in return for 20 percent of the profit. He jumped at the chance and I started on my next journey: owning apartments. I started with 36 units in Wisconsin and found out I loved the business. In early 2003, I "bet the farm" again, and within three months I sold my financial planning practice, my house and all the furnishings, and the 36 units (at a loss), and my new wife and I moved to Orlando and bought a 90-unit apartment complex. Everybody was moving to Florida, so I figured it must be a good place to own property. I was right—eventually. That first property was the hardest we would ever manage. We fought through three hurricanes, two fires, and a huge learning curve, but in three and a half years we sold all of our Florida properties for a gain of over $2 million. I took the profits from Florida to buy the 600 units we now manage in North Carolina. My firm, Carolina Parks, has an annual rental income of over $3 million, only four employees, and property worth more than $23 million!

So, now I wake up and walk ten steps to my awesome home office in our beautiful North Carolina home. I work (if you can call it that) 25 hours a week at most, have great residual income, and most importantly, I control my own time. I can focus on my family, pursue my passion of golf, and continue life coaching.

I am grateful to be living the life I love!

Micheal B. Conlon, J.D.

FROM WAITING TABLES TO TRAVELING THE WORLD
Steven Nicolle

Have you ever wished you could travel the world, work in a profession in which every day was a new beginning, meet interesting people, meet your future spouse or be an entertainer and get paid for it? Would you like to do these things with an average amount of knowledge and experience but lots of desire? Well, here is my story.

I was a shipper, receiver and truck driver for a pharmaceutical company and, after having gone from job to job from ages 18 to 21, I came to the conclusion that I was not happy in my work life.

I later learned that doing something over and over again and expecting a different result was the definition of insanity. While I didn't know that at my young age, when I saw an advertisement for a bartending course, I knew it was my ticket to something different.

I immediately loved it. One night each week I learned to mix any beverage you could imagine. I even bought the alcohol to practice at home, making drinks for my mother. During the course, I met the manager of a pub and he hired me immediately.

Although the job was short-lived—he sold out and the new owner laid me off—I got a service bartender position at a name-brand hotel in Toronto shortly thereafter. I had worked in Toronto before, and had kept in touch with someone who was working in hotels at the time. After two weeks, he called me and I was hired as a bar manager in a private golf club. With only about a month's bartending experience, I was already a bar manager!

The next couple of years I went back and forth, working at a few different places and learning the bartending trade as I went along. After about four years in the industry, I took a home study course in hotel and motel restaurant management while working as a bar manager in Montreal. I was 26 years old and had an apartment, but I was unsure if I was ready to settle down in one place. For those of you wondering the same thing: if you are not ready to settle, don't!

As soon as I received my diploma, I decided I wanted to tend bar on a cruise ship. I sent my resumé to all of the cruise lines I could find.

While at work one day, I got a call with an offer of employment from the largest cruise ship in the world, the SS Norway out of Miami. I jumped at the chance and gave my two weeks notice. Days later I was in Miami embarking on the big ship. The job lasted only two months. It was not the experience I expected, as ship life is different from working on land. But if I didn't try, I would not have the experience. Later in life this experience proved invaluable.

I returned to Montreal still unsure if I wanted to settle down or not. I decided I wanted to learn French and enrolled in a six-month class. While there, I met someone who suggested that I work in Switzerland through a Canadian/Swiss exchange. I applied, was accepted and proceeded to send out 52 resumés to the French-speaking area. I received 26 replies and one of them was a "yes."

At 29, I left for two beautiful years in Switzerland. I traveled all over the country, and saw most of France, Italy, Germany and Austria, while getting experience as an assistant food and beverage manager.

During my last year there, I went to an interview for a new cruise line that was just starting, but my contract in Switzerland conflicted, so I was not able to start on the new opportunity.

After my stint in Switzerland, I headed back to Canada and then off to England to work as a restaurant manager, gaining even more experience and seeing the world.

I was in England for a year before heading back home, where I went to work in the Canadian Rockies for a year. I worked as a waiter and, after the restaurant closed for the season, began looking for work abroad once more. This time I was selective in my choice of cruise lines and sent my resumé only to the smaller ones. Do you remember that interview in Switzerland I told you about? Well, they hired me, and for the next four years I worked in Asia, Africa, the Caribbean, the Mediterranean, the Indian Ocean, Scandinavia and Russia.

I participated in the cruise show every week, singing my rendition of "My Way" by Frank Sinatra and "Singin' in the Rain" by Gene Kelly. I have served such celebrities as Pierre Elliot Trudeau, Prince Philip, the oldest survivor of the Titanic, the King of Sweden and the remaining members of the Mamas and Papas on the SS Norway—I was even invited for a sing-along in their cabin the last night of the voyage.

All of these experiences came about from a 15-hour bartending course taken years before. Who would have thought an average guy like myself would have such tremendous experiences? All I had to do was think about what type of life I wanted and figure out how to get it. Trust your own intuition and never dismiss anything as insignificant. That one thought could change everything.

 *Steven Nicolle*

ABUNDANCE HAS NEVER BEEN IN SHORT SUPPLY
Jay Westbrook

There have been three distinct phases in my life, each filled with a very different kind of abundance. For me, the question has never been about the presence or absence of abundance, or even the *quantity* of abundance. Rather, it has been about the quality of that abundance and its effect on the quality of my life.

Childhood Abundance
As a child, beginning at the age of three, I was a victim of long-term, brutal, multi-perpetrator sexual abuse accompanied by beatings, followed by being thrown into a pitch-black closet to sleep. I was also physically abused by a violent and inconsistent mother. We moved 16 times during my first 11 years of school, and my parents drilled into my head that there was no God, that poor families like ours had no chance of success and that money and those who had it were evil.

Therefore, my childhood was characterized by an abundance of terror, violence, brutality, isolation, secrets, lies, hopelessness and fantasy. My life had little quality, and was focused simply on enduring the pain until I was returned to the physical safety of the dark closet, only to be consumed by an emotional terror of the total darkness. I learned that my only value was as an object of abuse, that I did not get to say "no" or set any boundaries, and that as difficult as the sexual and physical violence were to endure, they were preferable to the loneliness and terror of the dark closet.

Teenage & Young Adult Abundance
As a teen and young adult, I engaged in behaviors that validated my beliefs about my self-worth. I was angry, selfish, unappreciative and suffering, though unwilling to acknowledge that suffering. I was so damaged by my childhood that I was suicidal. Then I found drugs and alcohol; they mitigated the feelings, but led to stupidity and poor decisions.

Those decisions put me in front of a judge who sentenced me to double "five to life" sentences in the state penitentiary.

Upon release, I found myself broken and deficient on every level—spiritually, emotionally, physically, financially and educationally (I was a high school dropout). I had no ambition or self-esteem. I vowed not to return to prison, but set about constructing a self-imposed prison of my abundance of character defects.

This period was characterized by an abundance of self-pity, blame, shame, worthlessness, anger, self-sabotage, self-hate, hopelessness, fear, bitterness, envy, fantasy and irresponsibility. In short, I was not a vision, and the quality of my life was what one might predict for anyone wallowing in an abundance of these character traits.

Opportunity sat patiently in front of me while I continued to focus on my past and hone my skills and identity as a victim. Then, a friend suggested to me that "if nothing changes, nothing changes," and that I needed to do something—anything—differently. It hit me like a ton of bricks: I could continue to have a life filled with an abundance of misery, or I could change. I had a great place from which to start: sick and tired of being sick and tired, out of plans, little to lose and willing to take direction. Wounded and suffering, I was unaware of how that suffering could become a vehicle to awaken compassion in me, for me and for others.

Today's Abundance
That compassion allowed me to become a wounded healer, working with dying patients and grieving families. My bachelor's and master's degrees, followed by a certificate in counseling and being licensed as a Registered Nurse, provided education and credentials. After years as a hospice nurse, I had the opportunity to serve as clinical director of the first Palliative Care & Bereavement Service in a California community hospital. In that role I have won many national and regional awards,

and more importantly, served thousands of patients and families as they approached the end of life.

I have not had to return to the stone and steel penitentiary, nor the self-created one of my hopelessness and character defects. Rather, I have embraced a life of service that has carried me to Harvard Medical School (as 2005 Visiting Faculty Scholar), to Capitol Hill (for a national award) and to "Nurse of the Year." I even got to return to prison to teach "Being With Dying" techniques to the inmate volunteers of the prison hospice; and I got to walk out the doors at the end of that training!

I have unwaveringly been of service to the dying and grieving—the work I love. While continuing my clinical responsibilities, I have created Compassionate Journey, an end-of-life education and consulting service that empowers me to share with others my heart and expertise.

My life today is characterized by an abundance of grace and opportunities to serve. I have a tender and loving long-term marriage to my wife, Nancy. We live in a lovely Southern California home with a pool, guesthouse and our four Coonhounds. I live in the moment, walk with faith, do the work I love, earn an excellent living and I am comfortable in my skin; I am at peace.

My work with the grieving and dying fills me with gratitude, changes my perspective, provides amazing opportunities for service and reminds me to walk with a soft belly, an open heart, a posture of exploration and a certainty that the place where life and death meet is filled with God.

Yes, I used the "G" word. Actually, I discovered a fellowship of people who seemed happy and successful, but assured me they had been neither of those things in their individual pasts. They were spiritual, not religious, and were willing to share, for fun and for free, that which had facilitated their change. They told me that what had happened to me as a child was not my fault, but that what I chose to do with those experiences was entirely my responsibility, and that neither blame nor self-pity would improve my life. They suggested that self-esteem would come from doing esteemable acts, that I needed to go through the doors that were open, and that—since we see what we look for—I needed to look for solutions, not problems: for what was right—not what was wrong.

In taking these simple directions, the abundance in my life has changed. The abundance of misery, suffering, hopelessness, worthlessness and self-sabotage of my past has been replaced. Today I live with an abundance of mercy, grace, service, love, humility, humor, freedom, gratitude, compassion, generosity, tenderness, gentleness and contentment. I would not wish my childhood on anyone else, but I am so grateful for it. The suffering of my past became my vehicle for awakening compassion, and compassion the vehicle of my transformation. I am grateful for my life—a life filled with blessings and abundance.

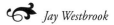 *Jay Westbrook*

AWAKENING
Weston Headley

One night she didn't come home. She had been with another man, which turned out to be a symptom of something larger. What I thought had been a mutually happy relationship was just a façade.

Since it had been a long-term relationship, it took months before the final blow was struck, and I came home to an empty apartment. Plans of marriage and children together—once a source of joy—became painful reminders of what had been lost.

To add insult to injury, during this ordeal I was in such an emotional state that I made huge business and investment mistakes, which cost me a significant chunk of my modest wealth. This didn't feel like a temporary setback; these were feelings of irrevocable loss and permanent pain, and yet, they weren't new. In fact, these feelings seemed vaguely familiar.

Old fears, deep-seated in a childhood of poverty and constant relocation, reared their ugly heads so clearly that I couldn't ignore them anymore. It became clear to me, in my empty home, that those fears had been lurking like a low-grade fever in my spirit and everyday habits for years. To see these old fears in the clear light of day was a blessing that changed my life. But, first, I had to look straight at two specific fears and their age-old grip on me. It didn't take years of therapy to see this— a few weeks of candid discussions with loved ones and with myself did the job.

One was a fear of poverty, the other of alienation. These fears weren't surprising, since I had grown up on welfare in an outcast family that moved frequently. I was always the "new kid at school" from the family with whom no one interacted. Determined to escape, I always worked hard at school. Eventually I received scholarships to Stanford University for both undergraduate and graduate degrees. In college, I worked hard to build a network of friends who became something of a surrogate family for me.

Years later, making well over a quarter of a million dollars a year and with a circle of wonderful friends, it was easy for me to believe that I'd overcome my past challenges. I was no longer poor or alienated, but the fears of slipping back into poverty and being alone had not died. Even as my outer world changed over the years, my inner demons stayed the same, sapping my energy and dulling the joy of life. Recognizing this was the first phase of my awakening.

Now that I had identified my fears, it was time to uproot them. I read the standard set of personal development books—all of which highlighted the need for gratitude for what I already had. However, I knew relying wholly on experts wasn't appropriate; this was my work and I needed to take ownership of it. I drew upon my business experience as a management consultant, helping companies to develop strategic plans and to manage the change necessary to execute those strategies.

Three lessons that I taught business clients were clearly applicable to my personal journey. First, I had to be strategic and focus on my long-term objectives. Second, I needed to break initial momentum with small and immediate wins. Third, I needed to focus on my migration plan. Rather than expect to carry out a detailed plan, a migration plan recognized that much could be learned in the course of "island hopping" from one small win to another. Having this plan for managing change was the second phase of my awakening.

Now it was time to execute. I began dating and re-engaged with old friends. My social life became richer than it had ever been before, even without a serious relationship. I had an epiphany: I didn't need to worry about being alone. Instead, I had to focus on settling for nothing less than what I deserved. Suddenly, the old fears and doubts had turned into quiet confidence.

This new-found confidence quickly migrated to my business life. I began to consider a wide range of career changes, no longer afraid of talking to people about them. At each turn, I was offered wonderful advice and new opportunities.

To make a long story short, I began two new businesses in which I worked with others to innovate, build and, in turn, help both individuals and organizations. The compensation was far better than anything I dared to dream of before. My financial losses now seemed so small that I couldn't help but laugh at those old fears of poverty. More importantly, I know that even if I had to start from scratch tomorrow, I could do it all over again and have a blast doing it!

Perhaps best of all, during the migration phase of shifting from my old career and exploring new opportunities (which lasted well over a year), I began to appreciate my old business and day-to-day work so much more. The weight of fears lifted and I could relax enough to appreciate that I had already built a pretty good career—wonderful clients, interesting work, good compensation and flexibility that often allowed me to work from my back patio or the neighborhood park. I also had the flexibility to spend more time with the people I cared about.

The fog of fear removed, I awoke to what I already had—wonderful friends and great career. At the same time, I imagined and began building an even better life. With the weight lifted from my spirit and my energy recharged, I've not only accomplished more and played more, but I have the energy to give more to friends and family—more support, more love, more of my spirit.

My journey happened to begin with what appeared, at first, to be a disaster. Yet, I could have identified my fears without losing a relationship and a ton of money. The recipe was simple:

1. Step back and honestly evaluate your fears and shine light on them.

2. Develop a plan to uproot them, drawing upon your own skills and experience, as well as lessons from the lives of others.
3. Start taking even the smallest steps to change the habits and assumptions associated with those fears.
4. Watch the momentum grow. Don't worry about temporary setbacks, as that gives the fears an opportunity to take root again.

I found that a few things can result from this weeding out of fear: 1) You might awaken to the fact that you already have a wonderful life and really need only to start appreciating it more, which is easy if you're not burdened with irrational fears, 2) you might set out on the path to build a life so wonderful that you couldn't have imagined it in the fog of fear, or 3) you will enjoy both possibilities by appreciating your current life while building an even better one.

With the fear of fog lifted, there is abundant beauty to behold!

Weston Headley

WHO'S COUNTING?
Scott Ercoliani

One

There I was, 7 years old, playing with a neighborhood friend. We played together often and let our imaginations fly. What fun we had; we were free, with joy in our hearts—most of the time. On this particular day, we started to argue. I actually forget what the argument was about, but I do remember I wanted things to go a certain way—my way, not his. Well, he wouldn't have any of that. He shoved me down, jumped on top of me and pushed my face into the ground. I'll never forget it. I can remember the rough feel of the dirt and gravel smashing against the side of my face.

Now, as a grown man looking back, the event doesn't seem so earth-shattering; just a small boy pushing another boy's face into the ground. But that event changed my life. In that moment I decided something— I decided, "I am weak." Since then, I have spent most of my life trying to prove how strong I am.

Two

I remember, as a young karate student, being trained by Sensei Campos, one of the few 5th degree black belt karate instructors in the United States at that time. I'll never forget: before each lesson, we would begin by kneeling and slowly closing our eyes to meditate—letting go of all worry, stress, concern and struggle—and relaxing into the moment. He explained that during this process we prepared our mind, body and spirit for our work that day. He said this was a sacred time and place where only free-flowing, peaceful thoughts could exist. He told us not to worry and assured us that our problems, if we so chose, would wait for us outside the gates of that sacred place. After we completed the lesson, we could meet up with them and perhaps greet them with newfound energy—a fresh perspective. For now, we would have to leave them behind. I discovered that the problems, if there were any, somehow seemed less significant by the time we were finished. I think he knew all along. I now see it is important to be intentional and bless the space and time we enter. I apply this practice today as often as I can by becoming present to the precious gift of life—excited and anticipating my next move toward joy, freedom and abundance. When I begin a day by honoring it as a sacred space, it makes all the difference in the world. Everything flows with ease. The world becomes a sacred place.

Three

I love movies—always have, always will. When I saw the movie Rocky, I was lit up with inspiration. Here was a story of a simple guy from Philadelphia who became a world-class boxing contender. At that time in my life I was training for karate tournaments, so I was ripe for inspiration from a movie like Rocky. Maybe this isn't one of your favorite movies. Maybe it didn't inspire you the way it inspired me. It doesn't really matter. What matters is that it inspired me so much that I was drinking raw eggs, wearing a towel around my neck and tucking in my sweatshirt while jogging for miles in my neighborhood. I'd even get a "hello" from some of the neighbors, just like in the movie. I remember Mr. Simon yelling out the window of his silver Eldorado, "Go, Scotty, go," as he drove by. All I heard was, "Go, Rocky, go!" And boy did I ever; I trained hard and I was inspired. I won many New York state tournaments in my division. Later that year, I was invited to compete at the Martial Arts Rating System's National Championship and I took first place. Shortly after that, I earned a Shodan 1st degree black belt. I began teaching two classes for children each week. We would begin each class on our knees, creating a sacred space—a sacred place to learn, grow and enrich our lives through the discipline of practice.

Four

When I first met my wife, Kim, 15 years ago, I had no idea she and her two sons, Jason and Mitchell, would have such an impact on my life. I knew I wanted to be with Kim, but I was afraid of including the boys. I didn't know how to raise two boys. They were 7 and 8 years old and I was glad when I learned they would be living with their father. Kim and I would have the boys on holidays and during the summer. We had a great time when we were together. It reminded me of the fun times I had growing up with my dad. But I always knew they would leave soon to go back to their home, with their real father. That was just fine with me. The thought of having to raise them scared me to death. I thought I would ruin their lives—I didn't know how to be a father. Could I afford it? Could I handle all the stress? I didn't want to try.

Time went by; the boys would come and go. Everything was fine until I began to wake up to the fact that my wife wasn't very happy. Naturally, she wanted her boys to be with us—permanently. The time had come when what I had resisted and feared was literally at my doorstep: the boys moved in with us. Much to my surprise and delight, I fell in love with them; I became the richest man in the world. These guys are my buddies—forever.

I'll never forget when Mitchell, the youngest, invited me to parent's night at the local high school basketball game. He was quite a player—one of those team players who often set up the other guy to take the shot. Kim was unable to attend, so there I was at the game with all the other parents, watching my boy play ball. At half-time I was called out onto the court. I'll never forget Mitchell running out on the floor to greet me. He had a rose in his hand. He gave me the rose and hugged me, grabbed me by my shoulders, looked straight into my eyes and said, "Scott, thank you for being here for me. I love you." I stood there for a moment smiling, as people from our community applauded in the bleachers. And in that moment, as I embraced my boy, I knew what it was like to be a proud father. All I could do was smile. Now, that is rich. That is abundance.

Counting My Blessings
Living a life I love in abundance starts with being grateful for the people

in my life. I am the richest man in the world because of my childhood friends, my family, my teachers, my wife and children, and my community. I am abundantly happy.

Scott Ercoliani

AN UNUSUAL LIFE
Art Solis

I have lived an unusual life!

I have had three car accidents and have been paralyzed twice. I was once hit by a car while riding my bike. I have lost more than 100 people I knew personally in a 43-year life span. These friends and family members who have passed on have ranged from infant to 90 years of age. It was with honor that I was able to sing at most of their funerals.

I grew up with 35 kids from my neighborhood and surrounding areas, including some of my brothers and sisters. I have a brother who is 18 years older and a sister who is 20 years older. I have never lived with either of them. They moved out of the house before I was born. My sister and mother were pregnant at the same time—how crazy is that? We lived in a nice neighborhood, two blocks from the park, three blocks from school and three blocks from the grocery store. I did not have a boring childhood, nor did I ever know hunger or lack. My parents were not rich, but they knew how to save. We always felt abundance.

I have been a locksmith for 24 years, and a singer, songwriter and musician for 27 years. I have taken my music to Thailand, Spain, England and many cities in the United States as a Christian music missionary, sharing the stage with popular artists. I have two CDs, *Art Solis and Friends* and a children's CD, *For the Little Ones*. Some of my songs are being played on Christian radio today. I have also been a ventriloquist for eight years. I enjoy making people laugh. I have held many different jobs from working with airplanes to sales to security work.

I pursued all of these jobs because I thought they would bring joy and happiness to my financial life, but they never did. Some people in my family have become celebrities—from a congressman and a television anchorman to a cousin who plays guitar with the singer Usher. I have met and spent time with some of the most famous country singers who have ever lived. I could write an entire book about my family and the things that have happened to us. I tell you these things not to brag, but because the only thing I cared about through it all was the Christian music ministry—all the other stuff was unimportant to me. I found my own abundance.

In the early part of May 2007, I was off work following a car accident. After watching a television show about success, I went to the Web site they had given to read more about the man who was speaking and the books he had written. As I was looking over the Web site, I saw a book that caught my attention. It was called Billionaire Secrets to Success by Bill Bartmann. I heard a message from Bill Bartmann on "The 9 Keys to Success" that redirected my life forever. One of the keys that hit me like a ton of bricks was to make sure my dream was my own—not someone else's.

So I thought about my passions and pursued them. I have always loved to write books, and I now have five books completed, three books in the making and, of course, this book that you are reading. I have never thought about writing for a living until now! Because of Bill's message, I am focused on what I am passionate about—winning souls for the king-dom of God and writing books that will help others.

It's sad that there are so many people who die with unfulfilled dreams. Anyone can change his own situation and accomplish his goals. Any person who has become a millionaire or billionaire had to learn how to become one. Those to whom it was given had to learn how to keep it. Learning is all that is required. If you learn how it is done, then you, too, will reach the same success. You have heard it said: "Knowledge is power."

I have seen many miracles by the hand of God in my life and my part in this book is one of them. I love writing about things that help people! Not only do I enjoy it, but now, I am living it! The fact that you are reading this story is the result of my re-focusing my direction from a life of feeling abundance to a life of knowing abundance. I know as I pursue my dreams I will continue the awkward stage, learning to write, before I reach the instinctive stage of writing where success lives. I know that friends, family and others will help me achieve my success, but only if I do my part—focus, dedication and constant learning. This is what I will do for the rest of my life!

With anything you want to learn in life, you must pass through those three stages. You can't skip one to get to the other. You must go through them one at a time. Nothing is too hard; people need to understand that learning is awkward at first, as when you first tried to walk or ride a bike.

Why pursue something that doesn't make you happy? I believe it is a waste of time! Pursue what you know you love to do and what brings joy to your heart—not what brings stress. I ask you, my friend, who said that you can't? Remember—one idea with passion, put into action, can create an avalanche of wealth. This is what is taking place in my life! Glory to God!

 Art Solis

Don't Forget to Say "Thank You"
Phil Shafer

Like many others, I was always searching, testing and looking for that chance to transform into something—hopefully something better. I've learned a lot of things over the years this way, including one of my favorites: how to get a parking place anywhere, anytime, especially when you really need one. It's an example—small but important—of manifesting the abundance of the universe. Still, it's a good place to start. Take little steps (do small things first) to gain experience in how the world works.

I believe we are all on this earth to learn to discipline our thoughts and actions so we can carefully and consciously manifest our dreams. A parking place may seem small, but it tones and flexes a muscle many haven't used in a long time, if ever—the muscle of manifestation—and it takes a bit of focus and intent to make it work properly.

The universe is like a short order cook: It takes our thoughts as orders and proceeds to crank out the dishes as quickly as it can. Depending on the thoughts and the person doing the thinking, the dish can taste pretty sweet. Other times, not so much.

The universe is like a master carpenter: With an infinite supply of tools and materials, it is always listening to your thoughts and running down the road just ahead of you to bang together the reflection of your dominant thought forms. Again, depending on the person and their thoughts, that reality may be nurturing and pleasant. Other times, it isn't.

The universe is an infinite field of potential outcomes that interacts with each of us to manifest whatever we think and believe. Be careful what you wish for and remember: Whatever you think and believe will become true for you. Since we've all heard this advice before, it might be more useful to figure out how to use it. It takes practice at visualizing and focusing our thoughts to manifest that abundance, and it's going to take something to practice on to get our manifesting muscles to feel a success, and thus gain experience and confidence in its use. That's where parking spaces come in. Remember, it's a lot easier to practice small steps now and be ready for the bigger steps later than to try to run a marathon without any training.

So here's the tool; each reader gets to be his or her own carpenter.

Parking Spaces—Anywhere, Anytime, as Close as You Want:
Before leaving your home…

1. Take a few relaxing breaths.
2. Close your eyes.
3. Visualize yourself driving up to and parking in an open parking space as near or far from your destination as you wish. Obviously, closer is better, but you might want to just ease into this practice and work your way up to a space right in front of the door.
4. Once you've visualized the space your car is parked in, imagine how good it will feel when it happens.
5. Get that in your mind, feel it in your body, and now forget it. Put it out of your mind, get in the car and go on over. Don't drive to your destination thinking about whether or not there will be a space. Put it out of your mind and let the universe manifest a parking space in the manner you visualized. Trust the universe to take care of it.
6. Now—this is very important—when you find the parking space right where you visualized it, don't freak out! Just park the car, say "thank you" and be happy. You have interacted consciously with the universe and actually manifested something.

Once you have mastered parking spaces, then who knows what else you might be able to manifest? Remember, the key concept you need to learn is how to discipline your thoughts and how to focus on things that are positive and nurturing. Thinking and focusing on unpleasant things has a way of manifesting in our lives as well. I know, because that was my mistake. I had one of those really small, negative thoughts and threw it out into the universe on several occasions when I said to friends in Santa Fe, "Oh yeah, we're moving to Mississippi so we can be closer to family and be wiped out by a hurricane." Eight months later, Hurricane Katrina took everything we owned.

Change your thoughts to change your life before your thoughts change your life in ways you don't expect.

 *Phil Shafer*

ABUNDANCE OR CLUTTER – YOU DECIDE
Dr. Marilyn Robinson

*T*he *American Heritage Dictionary* defines abundance as "a great quantity; plentiful amount; fullness to overflowing." A cursory Internet search for "abundance" yielded approximately 44,600,000 sites. While some sites focused on abundance from the perspective of areas such as chemistry, ecology, computer programming and economics, sites touting the acquisition and retention of personal abundance appeared to take center stage.

Abundance, like money, is neither inherently good nor bad. It is the way in which we pursue abundance and what we do with it that determines whether it results in value added or value lost. Abundance can take many forms, not just economic and material. Desired abundance can encompass extraordinary relationships, vitality and emotional well-being, to name a few. Abundance can be like a moving target—just when you think you've attained it, something else appears on the horizon. Abundance can also be an internal state of love, knowingness and joy. This internal state need not diminish with time or circumstance, but can be maintained and enhanced depending on your beliefs, values and principles.

We live in abundant times; America's pursuit of "the good life" has lead to expanded waist lines and homes overflowing with material goods. Our world is filled with marketing messages that encourage and subliminally foster the constant acquisition of external symbols of abundance. Could it be that we have used our precious resources of time, money and focus in a way that has deprived us of intangible, priceless assets? Could it be that, in the pursuit of abundance, we have cluttered our lives?

The American Heritage Dictionary defines clutter as "a confused or disorganized state or collection; a litter; a jumble." Clutter's impact on the intellect can be noted in the many messages and thoughts competing for our attention, potentially undermining our clarity and focus. Being surrounded by clutter can drain energy and create a state of confusion or indecisiveness leading to or increasing procrastination, anxiety, depression, fear and learned helplessness. So, what is the relationship between abundance and clutter?

For me, abundance has always been about the things to which a price tag cannot be attached. I experienced abundance early in life. As the oldest daughter and second of 12 children, I lived in an environment abundant with family, friends, love and activities. I had great clarity about my career path due to the great number of amazing people in my life who modeled excellence and compassion. Through school and church I had the opportunity to contribute and volunteer, giving me a diverse skill set and the confidence to live outside my comfort zone. I experienced abundance in the many career paths I chose, the educational opportunities, the limitless flow of ideas, the sense of well-being and confidence my parents instilled in me, and the unwavering certainty that I would always overcome obstacles. Then something happened that has given me greater awareness and compassion: I became acutely aware of the potentially insidious, destructive potential of abundance after the death of my husband, Frank. This menacing presence initially took shape in the abundance of paper which flowed into my home. When there were two of us, it was often a daunting task to keep up with the myriad of information and material, and now I was faced with handling this influx on my own. As the inflow of paper quickly exceeded the outflow, it overtook storage space and spilled into boxes, piles, suitcases and any other available space.

Organization has always been my strong suit. Given a pile of information or tasks, I can creatively and effectively handle both content and volume with amazing speed and clarity. People have recognized and sought my guidance in this aspect of life and business management. Suddenly, it seemed as if I had completely lost this ability in my personal life. I could not seem to part with the magazines, catalogs and other materials that had been of interest to my husband. I discarded quite a bit, but saved many things—initially sorted by type or source—for when I had more time for careful thought and consideration. This emotional lack of confidence generalized and widened to include my personal paperwork, which generated ever-growing "I'll do it later" abundance.

The task at hand would not have become so insurmountable had it not been for the abundance of other material things in our life. Frank and I had purchased and renovated a three-story brick school house, built in 1909. We had completed the majority of the renovation, but, many boxes and stacks of things still needed to be sorted. The abundant 6,500-plus square feet of space was expanded to include a four-car, two-story garage. The three-quarter acre lot had been transformed from a wilderness into a beautiful, landscaped yard with an abundance of trees, garden areas, small structures and grass, all requiring constant attention and maintenance.

My work hours were intense and required a lot of travel. Balancing all of the tasks that needed to be accomplished during my non-working hours became what seemed like the bane of my existence. All of this was exacerbated by an endless and unrelenting flow of challenges, including car problems, a broken well pump motor, roof leaks, flight cancellations resulting in missed appointments and commitments, and other people mishandling things with a frequency that seemed like the Twilight Zone.

Just thinking about the endless list of tasks could drive me to take shelter in the pale light of the TV, a mind-numbing computer game or comfort food. Worse for me, I started to distrust myself; I couldn't count on myself to come through and my home was a constant reminder.

It took a while, but I finally got it. I had to stop and really think about what I was doing, where I was headed, what I truly valued in life; about how everything added value or detracted from my purpose. I needed to understand my situation, get clarity about my future and welcome less-than-perfection in my life. I bit the bullet and did the hardest thing—at least for me: I stopped. I stepped down from some leadership roles and started saying "no" so that I could create the space and time I needed to reinvent myself and my environment in a way that would support my future, not hinder it.

Decisions and actions come so easily when there is clarity of value and purpose. I am so grateful for the abundance of lessons I've learned and insights I've gained. I've always understood the importance of emotional state to the accomplishment of goals, but now I understand it on a deep, insightful level. Strategy paired with the acknowledgement of emotional readiness is not enough. It won't produce a truly extraordinary life.

The potentially paralyzing effect of abundant clutter, accumulating unnoticed, is not reserved for our personal lives. A similar pattern can be observed in business. An abundance of business clients, incoming calls and economic opportunities can easily pull our focus from the basics of our business plan and intent. Customers not valued, invention and creativity not pursued, and people not performing to their full potential all culminate in lost opportunities with impact far exceeding the obvious area of financial results.

It has been said that it is easy to get things started, and the person with true power is the one who can stop things or say "No." As you look around at your personal and professional life, do you see a reflection of what you value most? Or, as was the case for me, have you gone uncon-sciously AWOL and found yourself in a life that is not about what you value most? If so, do the hard thing: Stop. Get rid of the clutter. Harness the abundance you value and experience the resulting freedom and empowerment.

 *Dr. Marilyn Robinson*

ABUNDANT RETIREMENT? THINK AGAIN!
James F. Kurt

If I could show you how to live a wealthy lifestyle in retirement, never run out of money, minimize your taxes, create a powerful legacy for your children and not be a burden on those who love you, would you be interested?

Great, then pay attention! My goal is to provide clarity, balance, focus and confidence so that you, too, can achieve a healthy, wealthy lifestyle as you approach retirement.

You Deserve to Live an Abundant Life!
What does abundance mean to you? In my practice I have discovered that abundance is not a number. It is not a target. It is not the amount of money that you have stashed away in the bank. It's not your IRA or 401(k) statements or even the number of houses that you own.

Abundance is an *attitude*, a feeling that you get or a sense of calm that you possess when you know that you are in sync with yourself, your family, your dreams and your fears. When you can picture your future vividly in your mind and have taken the necessary steps to ensure that you are going to live the life that you love, it becomes easy to engage in life as an active participant!

It is About Choice and Control
You want it, you need it, and you may even crave it! The question is how do you get it?

If you know what "It" is, congratulations! If you have achieved "It," you have been truly blessed and I am happy for you. If you don't know what "It" is, then you need to keep reading.

"It" is about independence. When we have choices, we have control.

Too many of us either make bad choices or, even worse, make no choices at all. This only leads to others making the choices for you. Remember: The choices that others might make for you may not be the choices that you would make for yourself. Choose wisely and choose while you can. Take action! You *will* feel better about yourself. I guarantee it.

You might be thinking, "You don't really expect me to choose, do you?" If not you, then who? Now is the time for you to take charge and decide how and where you want to live your life. If you wait, the choices may not be yours to make. A few key questions to ask yourself as you approach retirement are:

- Where do you want to live? At home, or in a facility?
- Who do you want to make decisions for you?
- As you age, do you really want the government to decide your standard of living?
- Do you think that Social Security will be there for you? How about Medicare?
- What about your children? Do you want them to have to choose between you and their inheritance? It could happen, should you become infirmed and in need of long-term care or assistance with living.
- How are you going to afford to pay for the decisions you make?

Remember the "Golden Rule"
"He who has the gold makes the rules." It's sad, but true. This is the way the world works. If you have money, you have choices. *More money = More choices.*

We live in the richest country at the richest time with the greatest opportunities in the history of the world. Unfortunately, few of us know how to recognize opportunities or what to do with them when we see them.

You Don't Know What You Don't Know!

I sure didn't. I have an MBA from a university in Los Angeles that has a great football team. What I learned about how to manage money and assets for large multi-national companies allowed me to create tens of millions of dollars for those companies' stockholders. The tenacity, drive and winning spirit that was passed on to me by professors who actually created value for their clients was priceless. Unfortunately, what they taught me about managing my own money was, quite frankly, useless.

I didn't know what I didn't know. Whenever I tried to apply big-business strategies to my personal investments, my "trusted advisers" would get in the way. They would say, "People can't do that, businesses can." When you watch the news or read the paper, you see a steady stream of "experts" all touting variants of the same theme to the same group of people struggling to get ahead or just getting started.

Ride the Wave...Or Wipe Out

The U.S. Census Bureau estimates that 78 million baby boomers (born between 1946 and 1964) are headed for retirement. The Bureau of Labor Statistics estimates that a healthy male is going to live to age 85; age 87 for females. The fastest-growing segment of the population is made up of those over the age of 100. Are you prepared?

Have you set aside the funds you need to live abundantly for 20, 30 or 40 years after you stop working?

It's a tidal wave, and it is likely to head straight toward you! From sedans to suburbs, mini-vans to mutual funds, we 78 million baby boomers have accounted for virtually every major demographic and economic trend since World War II.

Now is the time for surfing lessons. Don't let this wave wipe you out!

The Directions are on the Outside of the Box

If you want to live abundantly, you must ask people who are already living abundantly how they did it. You cannot follow the advice given to the majority. They are in the same box that you are in, and the directions are on the outside!

Lessons for surfing the wave:
1. Stretch – Learn about investing, retirement and relationships.
2. Nourish – Understand what your assets are: Finance, family and relationships.
3. Don't go alone – Find real experts that you trust. They'll help when you fall.
4. Commit – Stick to it; soon your momentum will carry you.
5. Avoid the Rocks! – Know the dangers; avoid risky investments.
6. Enjoy the Ride! – Life is for living. Live the Life that YOU LOVE!

My sincere wish for you is abundance! I urge you to take action now to get on the road to freedom.

 *James F. Kurt*

Born to Share and Prosper
Barry Walter Boyd

Can you recall when you first became aware of yourself? The experience I remember was when I was approximately 18 months old. I recall seeing, hearing and even understanding a particular sequence of events even though I was so young. This memory has taught me that we all come into this world whole, perfect and complete. I'm still the same person I was then, as you are the same perfect you that you've always been.

Have you ever had the privilege to see consciousness awaken in a baby? At first there is the amazing little body, and then, suddenly, the soul shines through, looking out at the world for the first time. Next comes the sharing of a baby's cry, calling for help to those who are near. Our ability share is as innate as our very first breath. We were each born to share and to prosper as individual centers of our Creator; we are the most important creation in our universe.

We have been given everything we need to discover our unique gifts and talents, and to develop the skills that will help us to live up to our potential. Envision humanity choosing this as its common goal: to assist each individual to wake up and be the best that he or she can be. Imagine a world where we all pledge allegiance to our Creator and to planet Earth—our home with many faces, races and places, with excellent air, water, food, shelter and loving support for all.

This world can work for everyone. It has the potential to be heaven on Earth now—not sometime in the future—right now. We are the stewards of our abundant resources; we have dominion over our lives and our planet. It is up to us to choose the dreams we will make real.

The same creative intelligence that created you and me is still inside us. It is the intelligence within all seeds and everything is created from a seed. Every vision is a seed waiting to be planted into consciousness and tended until it begins to grow naturally into what it was designed to be.

Inside of every seed is a spiritual blueprint of what it can become. A kernel of corn has inside itself the ability to become a corn stalk. An apple seed knows how to attract what it needs from its environment to become a tree that bears fruit of its own kind. Everything that grows can produce many seeds that have the same ability to flourish and grow.

Our thoughts and visions grow in much the same way. Each thought contains a vision of what it can become. When we write down our visions and create plans to make them real, it is very much like planting a seed. From vision to thought to plan and then to the decision to make it so, we constantly use the creative process. It doesn't matter how big or small the idea; creation always happens in much the same way.

A vision without a plan shall remain only a dream, but a dream that is laid into a plan has the potential to grow into its design. That is why it is essential for every human to have a Living Life Plan™—so we know where we are going and what we are growing in our lives. If we know how heaven on Earth looks and feels, and how humans treat each other in this vision, then we can create the action plans we need to carry out each day in order to support this, too. The world can work for everyone.

There are many people on this planet who are already living a life they love and who have the ability to use the world as their abundant playground. They are buying houses, taking vacations and doing what they wish. You can do this, too, but first you need to have a plan. When you have a Living Life Plan™ and consistently take the steps to live the life you love, you will find yourself on the way to living your dream. We can learn to share and prosper by assisting other people in living their dreams as well.

There is also another side. There are billions of people struggling for mere existence every day. Their dream to have clean water, food, shelter, and the ability to pay their own way is out of reach. We can help them get these things.

As long as we can visualize heaven on Earth, we can head in the right direction. Let's make it our common goal to lead people, one at a time, in learning to design, plan and lead the lifestyle of their dreams. This is our job as humans. It is up to us—you and me. We are the only ones who can do it.

One of the main ingredients we all need is a product or service to offer others. What if there was a career available to everyone that could provide basic needs, including tools to help a person discover his or her talents and desires? We have created this new and exciting career for the people of planet Earth: a Career of Humanity™.

Can you imagine the abundant prosperity available to us when we focus on the things that support the future we want, instead of what we don't want? You and I make choices as we live in this world every day. We cast our vote for heaven or hell with every thought that enters our mind and with every dollar we spend. Join me in playing together and co-creating a world that works for everyone. I pray it is your dream, too—Share and Prosper.

 *Barry Walter Boyd*

LOVE THE LIFE YOU ARE LEARNING TO LEAD
Donald H. Wimmer, Ph.D.

"Wake up! Live the life you love!" might send a wrong message. If you already live it, this call is pointless. Otherwise, the point jabs at your lack. Loving a life you don't have is like looking at a half-empty glass; you feel emptied, unreal.

Decide to have the real, be what you feel. Love the real so your life—now only half full—can become a life "*full*-filled." Deep within you lies your secret, the fundamental orientation that shapes personal goals, attitudes and habits: your purpose.

Acquiring this awareness requires a deeper learning—a wisdom that enables you to see what underlies daily routines. Learn what you need to know to become aware of what it takes to lead your life. This learning will bring you to know an up-to-now unimaginable fulfillment. I put it this way: *Love the life you are learning to lead.* This maxim is the first of my secrets to living healthy and growing wealthy with peace of mind. I will give you two more of the 10 secrets, and then share with you three of seven major pitfalls that can lead you astray of your purpose.

Secret No. 2: What you do with what life gives you determines who you are as a person. The same was true of my mother. What she did with what life had given her determined who she (though deceased) is as a person.

I grew up on a farm in north-central Wisconsin, the ninth of 14 children. I never went to bed hungry, but I do remember mother occasionally saying that she didn't know where our next meal would come from. I always thought she meant she didn't know which garden to pick from; it never dawned on me how anguishing it must have been for her, but she always made us feel we had enough, giving us the sense of living in abundance, where affluence (having more than enough) isn't a requirement.

Secret No. 3: Live within your own sense of abundance by respecting others living within theirs. For the better part of a year, I watched an infant becoming a toddler. Lest I get in trouble with her mom, I watched the child closely and almost single-mindedly. I discovered that infants becoming toddlers don't just play. These "little Thomas Edisons," through trial and error, discover how to live in abundance—that is, until we adults start saying "No" to this and "No" to that. How long does it take to suppress the sense of living in abundance?

A newborn child is a clear glass of pure water. Every time the glass is jolted, a little water spills. You can imagine how much water has been spilled by the time they are teenagers. Adolescents come to resent authority in the shouts that replace true communication. Authority distills into frustrated force, probably due to inadequate adult attempts to outwit childish behaviors. Frustration defaults to force; force is not authority. Authority is life-giving. Force can kill; first mentally, then spiritually.

It is no wonder so many people have been conditioned to surrender their own quests for living in abundance. A little jolt tips the glass over. Once empty, what's left to lose? Temper! Put down the other guy, or immaturely taunt, tease or tantalize him.

An author's tasks are just the opposite: inform, invite and inspire. An author has the authority and power to render meaningful understanding of a given topic. For example, parents author their children's lives. Parental authority is the power to give that life meaning. Parents, above all, are responsible for teaching a child to appreciate learning to avoid pitfalls and to lead the life that they, as parents, are teaching their children to live. Authors who share this purpose share similar authority.

The Pits

Months ago, when I received the invitation to author a contribution to this collection, I first told myself to "Wake up and live the life I love!" Ha! I found myself looking at an emptying glass, draining all my unattended dreams. I definitely knew what I hadn't loved about my life these last few years: It was being steered by necessity—not by me.

At times, I felt that I just didn't like my life. It was not mine. I needed to learn to be free to lead it myself. Facing this writing opportunity put me through a three-month rewriting, self-defining and refining fire. I began to deal with the mess life gave me by working and re-working what "loving the life I am still learning to lead" was to mean to me personally.

For the past three years, my life has been subjected to a costly and constant distraction, tearing me away from achieving my purposes. I intended to gain personal wealth, to increase it with peace of mind, and to do that by helping others do the same for themselves. I want to share my experiences with you so you can derive valuable wisdom from them. Wisdom is learning from experience, especially the experiences of others.

Three Pitfalls

1. Trusting without verifying before putting ink to paper.
Don't even think of doing business on a mere handshake. Unlike older, simpler days, doing business on a handshake can be dangerously expensive. That mistake cost me thousands upon thousands of dollars a year. I don't want you to make the same mistake. I trusted, acted on that trust alone and made a BIG mistake; so, trust, but verify.

2. Falling into the euphoric mindset.
Could learning to lead the life you love seduce you into a heightened and exaggerated but false sense of easy achievability? There are a lot of programs out there that, compellingly promoted, create fantasies that appear so realistic that you jump right in. You put money into a course of action without *1) devising a plan, 2) allotting its needed time, and 3) without committing efforts to specific actions before dragging down your*

already overburdened credit. Money was all that was considered here because there was no plan, time, effort or action on the table anyway. How do you think I know that?

3. Overlooking due diligence.
This is the worst of all pitfalls: jumping to conclusions. It happens in all walks of life. You trusted, verified, devised a plan, but you did not spot the devil in the details.

Leading my life calls on me to take decisive action. At the right opportunity, I would launch my rocket and watch my wealth take off. I found it easy to do—coming out of a context of a large gathering with like-minded people—but I overlooked what I presumed to be a buyer's minor detail. Had I done my due diligence, I might have spotted seller deceptions. That's still open for an answer, but the resultant losses are without question.

To make a long story short, several months after "just one more" seminar three years ago, a few e-mail exchanges with a screener in Florida "qualified" me (or, more accurately, my retirement account) for purportedly "20 percent below market value" real estate purchases in Philadelphia. It was a package of six variously located row house units. In good faith, I shook hands with the seller and his network. I decided, I bought, and then I let the properties be managed by the seller's management company.

The initial shortfall became a downward plunge. Monthly deficits consistently ran over $2,000 due to missing income statements, double billing, faulty and deceptive repairs, and ultimately for reckless endangerment to the health and welfare of infant children, so I fired the management. Out of the frying pan and into the fire, I took over as manager, working directly with Section 8 and its protected tenants. Determined to be the best landlord, ever available to help them own their own homes if possible, what did I find? Unpaid utility bills defaulting to me as owner.

Friends tell me to get rid of these properties. I explain how shockingly overpriced properties would leave a pile of mortgages without their underlying assets to pay them down. I felt like I was being pushed toward a cliff—at the same time I felt as if I had already fallen into the pits.

Do I now start to claw my way out? Was this mess in my stars? Where's my horoscope? Is misery the destiny that deters me from doing what I really love? It is said that God writes straight with crooked lines. There's a particular kind of tree outside my window, the upper branches of which go off in every direction, yet the trunk, which cannot grow except from the roots underneath to the branches above, lives and grows straight and sturdy. My life has been something like that. Maybe yours has as well. The branches are what the trunk does with what it is given from the soil, sun and water. The advantages of being human lie in our unique ability to reflect, plan and take action. Who I am and who I will be, depends on what I do with what I have been given. What do I do when "life" gets in the way?

One night, as I lie there wondering what to do about everything, I took it apart and looked at each part. Then, overseeing them all together as if I were the CEO I learned that my foremost "job" is to learn the things my company needs in order to grow.

In other words, in accord with the E Myth, I need to work on my business, and not just get pushed around working in only part of my business. The love is in the learning, not just any learning, but the learning that leads to the right learning. The professional golfer loves learning to play golf better. That's what it means to be on top of one's game.

Learning is living and living is learning. He who stops learning, starts dying.

Love learning to lead your life; that is what I share with you. Fill your glass with an abundance that will overflow affluence and allow you to give back to the community, locally, nationally and planetwide

Donald H. Wimmer, Ph.D.

ON OUR WAY TO ABUNDANCE
Karen Wilson

I've learned the hard way that abundance can be tricky. Abundance is a perspective, a way of seeing the world and our lives in it. Because I used to associate abundance with "all good things," I always felt abundance during smooth-sailing periods of my life. But when hard times hit, I felt betrayed by the very concept.

When I was in my mid-20s I was diagnosed with scleraderma, a disease in which the protein in the collagen that lines your organs and muscles begins to harden and doesn't allow tissue to move or fluids to flow. At that time, more than 30 years ago, medical science knew very little about this condition, though it's now called an auto-immune disease. The doctors gave me this advice: "Do not have any more children and get your affairs in order." I was told I might have six to 18 months to live.

That very day—dazed, confused and terrified—I was trying to find my way out of the huge, underground medical center. Even though I had been there before, I got lost. I passed a darkened doorway and something caught my attention. It was some kind of equipment with a little screen that threw out soft, hazy light. I could barely make out the silhouette of a person standing next to the equipment. Bewildered, I asked, "What's happening in here?" The voice from the shadowy room said, "Bio-feedback." I thought out loud, "Hmm. I know bio means life, so does that mean that life feeds itself?" The voice replied, "I'm conducting research to show that people can change their blood pressure, skin temperature and heart rate by concentration."

"What?" I felt dizzy. I had just been told that science could not help me any further with the hard brown patches on my skin—they would grow, become worse, then I'd die—possibly soon. The hospital walls began to shimmer, my breath deepened, and I could feel myself light up, as if I was on fire. As the clinical sounds of the hospital faded, a firm, steady, knowing voice came from the deepest part of my being and stated clearly, *"If it*

is possible, I can do it." At the time, I didn't know how I would heal myself, but I knew that if thoughts and the way I use them could make those changes, if it was possible, then I could, and would, do it.

I took off on my own journey of traditional and non-traditional learning and training. I immersed myself in quantum science, indigenous wisdom, consciousness studies and Eastern knowledge. I became a healer, massage therapist, counselor, consultant and practical spiritual guide; basically, an expert at subtle communication. I discovered that I had been talking to myself through "survival thoughts," which I now call "Territorial Thinking." I would say things like, "If I do this, then the pay off is…" Without knowing it, I had been making deals with life! My thoughts had sprung from unconscious beliefs about competition and worries about not being "good enough." As I learned how to choose which thoughts to feed myself and became responsible for what runs my perceptions and reactions to life, a whole world of abundance opened up! Anything is possible. Nothing can exist outside a circle that encompasses *everything*. Awareness, attention and action, over time, can sculpt out paths for the river of abundance to flow.

I help people see where they're headed based on their patterned thinking. I help them to discover and overcome habitual thought patterns that unconsciously hold them back from living the life they love. Right now I'm in the midst of paying close attention to my own thoughts in a new way. My best friend and husband of 26 years died just four months ago. I gently weed out thoughts of self-pity and loneliness, and send forth waves of gratitude for having such great love in my life. Although it may take a heart of courage to stay steady and ready, abundance waits for you and me. We carry it in our bones, breath and blood. How do you answer Albert Einstein's famous question, "Is this a friendly or unfriendly universe?" If you perceive that you live in a friendly universe, then congratulations—you're on your way to abundance!

 *Karen Wilson*

FROM TERROR TO ABUNDANCE
Al Fury

I was petrified with fear. I was 24 years old and about to die. But death didn't scare me as much as the gruesome prospect of my body smashing into the rocks 225 feet below. I was standing on the precipice of a sheer granite cliff, about to jump. I had a choice as to how I wanted to die—quickly or slowly. I could refuse to jump and the Army brass at Fort Sill, Oklahoma, would wash me out of the Army's Officer's Training School and ship me promptly to the front lines of the Vietnam War as an artillery forward observer, where my life expectancy would be about 90 days; or, I could jump, and possibly survive long enough to graduate. I had acrophobia (an irrational fear of heights), and was more afraid of falling than I was of bullets. I was sweating profusely and sick with the knowledge that I would be humiliated, reviled as a coward, and lose all that I had suffered for if I froze now. It was called "rappelling"— descending great heights with nothing but a rope slipping through my hands to control my descent. What if I got rope burns and couldn't hold on, or my sweaty palms caused me to lose my grip? What if I panicked and lost my balance, or smashed into the face of the cliff and was knocked unconscious? Three officer candidates had already died doing this, so I wasn't overreacting. There was no net or soft sand on which to land. This was the real deal—nothing but jagged boulders.

I had made myself last in line. All of my classmates—119 of them—had gone before me, and were now standing at the bottom of the cliff, looking up at me in anticipation of my demise. Some were snickering devilishly. Some were seriously concerned for me. Many just didn't care and wanted to get out of the 105 degree heat.

I didn't think that I would make it, but I jumped. My body arched out over the cliff, the rope slipping through my hands. I crashed awkwardly into the side of the cliff, lost my balance and turned upside down but clung to the rope, dangling like a helpless jerk. The training officers yelled encouragement to me from the top of the cliff as I froze with heart-stopping panic. The blood was rushing to my head and I began to pass out. I realized that I would be dead for sure if I allowed that to happen. Somehow, I righted myself. The men below started to cheer for me, which instilled in me a new-found confidence. Somehow, I got to the bottom in one piece. I had made the grade, passed the test and conquered my fears—at least for the moment. But that's all that mattered: that moment.

I was overwhelmed with relief at first, and then a sense of pride and accomplishment set in. What was a difficult, but ordinary, challenge for the others was a life-changing ordeal for me. They had no idea how important that moment was for me. I had always been a pretty able person, but now I felt like Superman. Of course, that was the point of the exercise—to instill confidence and a sense of invulnerability—and it worked for me. In comparison to those chilling moments, facing gunfire or hand-to-hand combat was no big deal. I sailed through the rest of the training. Altogether, I spent 11 months in non-stop Army combat training and experienced multiple confidence-building moments before receiving my orders for Vietnam. But none were as gut-wrenching as that 225 foot sheer granite cliff.

When I returned to civilian life, I feared nothing. I dove into life with an exuberance that I had never felt before. I was married by then and wanted to do well for my wife and myself. I drove a school bus from 5 to 8 a.m. daily. Then, from 9 a.m. to 1 p.m. I attended classes at the local university. From 3 to 6 p.m. I taught high school math, social studies and physical education at a private Catholic school, after which I grabbed some dinner and sold real estate from 7 to 10 p.m. Every Saturday and Sunday I sold real estate all day. In essence, I never rested. After 18 months of this schedule, I had become the top salesman for my real estate company and was offered the job of sales manager. I didn't hesitate. I gave up school and my other jobs and threw myself into selling. Within eight months, I was vice president of the company. Two years later, I owned my own real estate company. I was fearless. I never looked back.

I should have known that being an entrepreneur was my destiny when I made my first small fortune at the age of 14. I was a military brat and lived with my parents all over the world. When my father was transferred to Japan, my family went with him. Japan was in post-war ruin in the early 1950s, and buildings were being demolished and re-constructed by the hundreds. Near where I lived, I noticed a demolition team stacking iron radiators in a fenced yard after removing them from a bombed-out building. After school one day, I went over and asked the superintendent what was to become of the radiators. It took me a while to understand what he was telling me in Japanese. "Scrap," was his answer. I asked if I could buy some of them for a project that I was working on. He said that he would ask the owners. The next day I returned and he told me I could buy as many as I wanted for 5,000 Yen a piece ($13.85 at that time). I feared that I might be getting in over my head, but I bought one anyway, thanked him and gave him a few bars of Ivory Soap. He was thrilled, but I was scared because I didn't know how I was going to move it or how much I could sell it for. I arranged to transport the radiator to a scrap yard where I sold it for the equivalent of $60 in America, and for the next 18 months I made two trips a week until the radiator yard was removed. I was sad to see it go. I had made almost $10,000 during my run, which in those days was a small fortune for anyone, much less a 14-year-old boy. Buying that first radiator could have been a fiasco, but I didn't let my fears stop me from doing what I had to do to succeed.

Although the granite cliff was my defining "wake up" moment, my radiator escapade was the most fun. I've had other "wake up" moments since then. I woke up when I applied for my first business loan and was declined because, as my banker told me, "You didn't ask for enough to complete your project." I had been afraid to ask for too much. Since then, I have helped thousands of business owners establish business credit and borrow enough money to make their dreams come true. My abundance has provided for theirs.

My message to you is not original, but it's urgent that you learn it! It's this: ANYONE can live the abundant life they love if they are bold and can face their fears, proving to themselves that fear alone cannot be allowed to stop them from doing what they have to do to succeed.

 Al Fury

FROM LIMITATIONS TO POSSIBILITY-LIVING
Florence E. Callender

At the age of 10, I read all the biographical books in our small town library. I told myself that I would be an author one day. I was intrigued with words; they held a magic key that unlocked doors to information and fed my seemingly insatiable hunger for knowledge. I loved to speak, but was too shy to do so outside of my very limited circle of friends. I also enjoyed writing, but was too afraid to do so, fearing that some inquisitive adult rummaging through my things would discover my unusual ruminations.

My quick wit and vocabulary impressed the members of my church and community, and the adults in my life verbalized their expectation that I would become "somebody extraordinary" when I grew up—meaning someone with a good, steady job from which to retire after 40 years. None of the prevailing professions impressed me. In fact, I hated them all. I wanted to be my own boss, work for myself, beat my own drum and dance to my own tune. But what profession could a girl have on a tiny island in the Caribbean Sea when all she wanted to do was read, write and speak? So whenever I was asked what I aspired to be, my planned answer was, "I don't know."

Life in St. Lucia was quite predictable. After high school, the principal encouraged my dad to send me back to teach. He said that at 16 I was too young to go straight to college. My dad agreed and I taught at my high school for three years. I hated every minute of it. Then came college. Having switched from business administration to education, I graduated with a Bachelor of Arts degree, still not knowing what I really wanted to do for my life's work.

Three-and-a-half years after graduation and yet another teaching job, I left the Caribbean and traveled halfway across the world, to California, to pursue studies in a hidden interest: fashion design. It was there that life became too painful for me to remain as shy as I was. So I became my own "special project."

I learned that "when the student is ready, the teacher will appear." Stumbling on the Nightingale Conant Corporation, I was introduced, via audio cassettes, to some of the world's great motivators—Jim Rohn, Les Brown, Wayne Dyer, Denis Waitley and Brian Tracy. My metamorphosis began. I changed from a shy, reserved student hiding in the back of the classroom to the salutatorian of my graduating class. While receiving a standing ovation at the end of my speech, I felt a slow-moving, bubbling spring of excitement rising up inside of me—I was on top of my world. My self-confidence soared—I could speak to hundreds of people and they would actually listen.

Working in Los Angeles was disappointing. An untrained imagination, budding self-confidence, the absence of a life map and ignorance of how the mind and the laws of the universe work are sure ingredients for sporadic success and living in reverse. I couldn't figure out how to stop renting my life out to help others fulfill their dreams while mine remained elusively submerged.

In January 1988, I moved to New York. Fear set in when I got to the huge city. I was a little fish in a big pond, and I was terrified. The words of my motivating mentors were long forgotten.

I struggled through each day as one disaster after another unfolded. I lived through relationship breakdown, loneliness, isolation, divorce, self-denigration and depression. It felt like I was hurtling uncontrollably into an abyss.

Then one day while browsing through television channels, I caught Oprah talking to a guest who was a life coach. Having never heard of that profession before, I sat riveted to the screen as she described what she did—how she helped other people hone their dreams and improve their lives. In that instant, I had a "light bulb" moment. I jumped to my feet, my heart screaming within me, "That's what I want to do!"

I took out my motivational tapes and began listening again. Another day, I turned my television set to PBS during a fund drive, and there was Les Brown giving a live workshop. Another time, while surfing the Net, up came SeminarsOnDVD.com and I found Bob Proctor's *Science of Getting Rich* DVD. Everywhere I turned, God sent someone to urge me forward on my journey toward discovering my purpose and designing my life around it.

I quit my job in the fashion design industry, went back to school and became a speech-language pathologist. Choosing to work in schools, I became an agent of hope, helping children see the possibilities that lie within them. For a couple of years, I succumbed to inertia and allowed my dreams to lie dormant. Then, in March of 2000, I was asked to speak at a school assembly. I woke up for the final time.

Enthusiasm and zest for living burned like fire in my bones. I realized that I am not only the canvas, but also the paint and paintbrush of my life. I didn't like the picture of my life, so I picked up the paintbrush and painted a different doorway to a new and more desirable life. I brought forth those early, God-given desires to speak, write and help others create the lives they desired. I soon became the resident motivational speaker at my school, and my colleagues started coming to my office to receive words of encouragement and inspiration.

Moving away from my life of self-imposed and conditioned limitations, I dared to take a step through my new doorway into my life of possibilities. I chose to believe that everything I need to live my purpose-driven, abundant life is already within me. Speaking appointments and coaching opportunities continue to roll in.

I accepted Jim Rohn's *challenge to succeed*. Brian Tracy instilled in me the importance of clarity of thought, and I pledged to prioritize my day using the *80/20* rule. I adopted Jack Canfield's *Hour of Power.* Bob Proctor gave me a visual representation of my mind and taught me the power of decision. I decided to begin living abundantly where I was, without knowing the details of how I was going to achieve my goals. I made the decision to change what I was doing in order to change the results I was getting.

As a Bible-believing Christian, I have held the words of Jesus Christ (John 10:10) in my mind for many years. He told us that He came so that we may have and enjoy life in abundance. I found out that we must first accept the abundance that is within us before it manifests outside of us. To get the pay, we must do the work. **Get ready** to wake up and live in your abundance: *Determine your vision, mission and goals.* **Get set:** *Make the road map—plan the steps.* **Go:** *Relentlessly pursue your goals.*

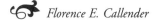 *Florence E. Callender*

ABUNDANCE AND RELATIONSHIPS: WHAT WE'VE LEARNED
Jesse Johnson & Melva Thomas Johnson

Some might question whether the subject of relationships should be included in a book about abundance. What do relationships have to do with abundance? Plenty! Keep reading and we'll explain.

A big part of the problem is that when most people think of abundance, they equate it with money—abundance means having lots of money. You've heard the phrase, "Show me the money." There is a commonly held belief that money is the ultimate road to happiness—you want enough to buy whatever you want. And some believe that it is acceptable to acquire money by any means necessary—be it legal or illegal—regardless of how many people are hurt in the process. This attitude of "I'm going to get mine no matter how it effects you" is demonstrated far too often by individuals at all levels in society—from desperate drug pushers in our most impoverished neighborhoods to corporate executives and politicians living in the most affluent communities. These people come from all walks of life.

This attitude is considerably different from the belief and value that we were taught as children. Our elders taught us that each of us is "our brother's keeper." They said that we are all somehow connected and that what we do with and for each other impacts all of our lives. As adults, we now see this concept as a profound universal and spiritual principle. Whatever I give to or take from others comes back to me in greater measure than what was given or taken. It's karma! This is also referred to as the Law of Compensation. It is quite simple: If you do good things for others, good comes back to you in abundance. If you do bad, harmful or thoughtless things to others, that also comes back to you—in abundance. It's the law! There is no escape!

If you believe that money alone will make you happy and you devote all your life to acquiring as much money as possible at the expense of so many other important things in your life, then you are likely to be sadly disappointed when you discover that the happiness you sought is not found in dollars.

We have known a number of wealthy people. Some of them handled their wealth well and were quite happy and content. They were very kind, loving, caring, giving individuals who devoted their lives to some worthwhile humanitarian cause. They wisely used their wealth to help others, and because they had discovered their life's purpose, they were contributing something of value to others. They were extremely happy and their lives were fulfilling. Others we have known handled their wealth poorly and were quite miserable. They were always preoccupied with their money. They were so fearful that they might lose it that they spent nearly every waking moment watching and worrying about it. They were not very happy, nor was it pleasant to be around them. Just how joyful or happy could they be? They lived in fear—fear that they wouldn't make money and fear that once they'd made it that they'd lose it. These individuals have no meaningful purpose—no mission other than making money. This is no way to live. Our hearts have gone out to such people and their families because we've seen the pain that their preoccupations with money have caused.

We have learned that true happiness is not so much about money or material things as it is about special moments in life that touch us in a particular way. For example, some of our happiest moments have come while the two of us have lovingly gazed into each other's eyes in a special moment of connection, or experienced the joy of holding a precious, innocent little baby in our arms. We love sitting together, enthralled with the beauty of a sunset, quietly engrossed in the sight and tranquil sounds of a bubbling brook, or sharing times of great fun, excitement, celebration and laughter with friends and family. Such moments are special. They tug at your heart strings. This is living—really living!

The bottom line for many of us is an intense desire to feel an abundance of love and caring that comes from a special connection with another human being. Personally, the two of us feel especially blessed to have the abundance of love we've found in each other, our sons, both sides of our families and numerous friends and colleagues. Each relationship enriches our daily lives in very specific, unique and special ways. We are filled with an abundance of joyous memories that we cherish. Whenever we recall these memories, those first wonderful feelings we had come flooding back to us so we can re-experience them again and again.

Without question, the quality of our lives is enormously enhanced through our relationships. Most of us would say that we are the most joyful and at our best when we feel a special, mutually satisfying connection with a significant other in our lives.

When we contribute to the well-being of others, we are in alignment with universal law. All forms of life—from the smallest organisms to the most complex—are interdependent. Each form contributes to the success of other forms of life. Humans represent the most complex form of life on the planet. When we align ourselves with our life purpose by contributing to the well-being of others, we experience the greatest degree of abundance. It may or may not necessarily be in the form of wealth. More important than money is the overwhelming sense of happiness we experience by knowing that we are making a contribution to others. When we live in alignment with this universal principle, we experience happiness, and our lives will be fulfilling and purposeful.

 *Jesse Johnson & Melva Thomas Johnson*

The Priceless Nickel
Ganada Kearney

There's a difference between surviving and living, and the majority of my life has been focused on surviving. Losing my parents and becoming a single mother by the age of 23 forced me to live in survival mode, and it's been a tremendous learning process for me. Needless to say, it has given me many life-lessons. I am thankful for most of those lessons; it is because of them that I am becoming a better person. Learning early on the importance of trusting God was the greatest lesson of all.

I recall a point in my life when a nickel was all the money I had in the world. I had a young child to feed, rent to pay and too much pride. How was I going to make everything work? I'm certain that if I had told my family the truth about what was really happening, they would have helped. But, I didn't. I felt that it was my problem, and it was my responsibility to resolve. I must admit, some of the detail escapes me, but I do remember that we were never homeless, never evicted, never had to live with anyone else, nor did we ever miss a meal. It might not have been what we wanted to eat, but we always had food. Little by little, I regained control of my finances by working a variety of jobs. It was at one of these jobs that someone suggested I go back to school.

Returning to school was one of the best decisions I have ever made. I received grant money and several loans to finance my education and to support my son and myself. Completing the certificate for Nuclear Medicine Technology took three years and made me eligible to take board exams. There were three different licensures, three different exams and three days of extreme stress. The time, money and energy put in were definitely wise investments. Upon passing the board exams, I returned to full-time employment, and with my first paycheck, we moved into a larger rental home in a nicer area. Things went well for more than three years until, to make a long story short, my landlord-tenant agreement changed and we were in a position in which moving was our best option. Upon taking the advice of a friend, I rented a small apartment a few blocks away for my son and me. The purpose was two-fold: 1) staying in the area meant that my son would remain in the same school, and 2) a smaller apartment meant less rent and more money to save toward buying my own home. For years I had talked about how much I wanted to be a homeowner, but one thing was missing: I had never taken steps toward accomplishing that goal. I had prayed about having my own home, but I hadn't done my part. Making a conscious decision to prepare by living on a budget was priceless. I now had a plan and I was actually excited about it. The more I saved, the more I wanted to save. I found ways to reduce my spending and still have money for us to travel and enjoy other activities. With a budget in place, I estimated that I could start looking at property within the year. But I was wrong—we had our own place in five months; am living proof that "faith without works is dead!"

A couple of years after buying my own home, I decided I would go back to school again. My son only had another year or so in high school, my finances were more stable, and I had too many accumulated hours not to get a degree. Besides, seeing a friend at work attending school full-time was the motivating factor for me to do the same. Working and attending school full-time was challenging, but once again, it was another wise investment. Having the support of my son, family and friends was very helpful. Hearing them cheer me on made me reach further. Over the next four years I completed two degrees and graduated with honors.

I had worked in nuclear medicine for 12 years and still enjoyed working in the profession, but I wanted to venture out. I began researching my options and, yes, prayer was a part of it, too. I knew that without God's guidance, all would be in vain. As time went on, I became discouraged because a great change didn't happen as or when I expected, but it did happen.

After trying other business ventures, I eventually became an independent contractor, providing my services in nuclear medicine. Choosing to go independent was very rewarding; I now have time and flexibility with my schedule.

While trying one of those many business ventures, I discovered a missing link: having the support of someone that was close to me. Having support can be quite beneficial. However, having someone close to you does not guarantee support. Such was the case in my last relationship. When I realized that I had let go of my goals, I was angry—not at him, but at myself. I had stopped dreaming, and this frightened me. It was time to regroup, and I did. For a while, I had to do the cheering myself.

Remembering the advice given to me by a friend, it was time to utilize my degree while I still had some youth! I became a volunteer mediator for the Los Angeles Superior Court. What a great way to utilize the degree and gain experience in the field! It has been rewarding working with attorneys and their clients.

The transition from surviving to living is an interesting journey. At the writing of this chapter, I am embarking upon a life-long dream of starting my own business! I am developing a mediation practice. The types of cases I have mediated thus far have varied, and I will retain much of that in my own practice. However, I plan to specialize in working with people who have property in foreclosure. I know what it took for me to become a property owner and I want to help other owners.

It's an exciting time, but a bit daunting as well. I am reminded of a famous quotation: "If you want to walk on water, you have to get out of the boat." Knowing the importance of doing my part—researching, developing a plan, praying and following through—the chain of events are already in motion. I have seen what happens when I put faith with my work!

Ganada Kearney

NOW HEAR THIS!
Lee Beard

You would have to agree that we live in a world of abundance in many forms, but one of the most obvious is the abundance of choice. No matter where you are in the world, you still have choices.

Before we explore our many choices, I must preface this story with my constant belief that we need a spiritual foundation in our life. For me, that is my belief in God. Then add the importance of physical health to allow you to enjoy the abundance that God provides. With that understood, let me offer two concepts that I feel make the abundance of choices a very beneficial part of life and success: perfection and the present.

Perfect

I recently met someone who introduced himself as being perfect. I joked that I try not to be perfect because people start to expect perfection from you. In reality, I do not expect to achieve perfection in this lifetime, but I was intrigued with his answer when he said that, in that very moment, he was perfect.

I had already discovered a wonderful concept in Jack Canfield's book *The Success Principles* where he says, "Create your future from your future." WOW! What a concept! This has had a tremendous influence on my thinking. Think about it: In your future, you have unlimited possibilities and unrestricted resources at your disposal. In your future, you do not have any mistakes. In fact, in your future, you are perfect.

Imagine what your perfect future looks like, and go get it. You do not have to be held back by your life today. If you want to make a change, do it; don't let anyone tell you that you can't. In the future, you can create a new, inspired you that you will be proud of, instead of living with old failures, disappointments, and the expectations or opinions of others.

In the Moment
Then I was reminded about the scene in the movie *The Peaceful Warrior* when the mentor told the student to "live in the moment." That comment has been helpful in reminding me to enjoy every moment and every blessing, each and every day. You can do amazing things when you block out distractions and live in the moment. Your life can completely change in one moment, so you should make it a change for the good.

The *Wake Up…Live the Life You Love* book series started when Steven E had a "wake up" moment; he heard a voice in the middle of the night that said, "Write a book!" This moment set him on a path that has had a positive impact on many lives around the world. By telling his story, he has encouraged others to remember and take action based on their own wake up moments.

I'm Back!
I have developed a phrase to remind me to stay in the moment; it seems to bring me joy just in repeating it. I just say, "I'm back!" So anytime I find myself wandering from the moment and letting the past weigh me down, I simply say, "I'm back!" I encourage you to try it as well and have fun with it.

I believe that living in the moment and creating your future from your future could have a profound, positive influence if you grasp these concepts and incorporate them into your everyday life. Just think: In your future, you do not have to carry anything from your past except what you want to have with you. If you choose, you can bring only the helpful, good, positive and loving experiences. Bring only the things that will be constructive to your life from this moment forward.

So, you have the choice to live in the moment and enjoy everything in the "now" along with the unlimited possibilities of your future. This very moment you can say, "I'm back," really mean it, and use it every moment of every day of your life. Build your best self starting now. It's your life. It's your choice. It's your future!

Lee Beard

AUTHOR INDEX

Matt Bacak began investing his first earnings at the age of 12, a young businessman in the making. Now, 15 years later, Bacak has survived failed businesses, botched partnerships, heavy credit card debt and bankruptcy—all in preparation for the accomplishments he has achieved today as a well-established Internet marketer and best-selling author. Matt Bacak became a millionaire at the age of 27. He currently is running three multi-million dollar companies and each company was built using the Internet.

Lee is a former television producer and business developer. He lives in Arkansas when not traveling as the co-creator of the *Wake Up...Live the Life You Love* book series. Lee is an author featured in more than a dozen motivational and inspirational volumes. He concentrates on bringing the power of the Wake Up network to bear on the challenges of business development. If you've had a "wake up" moment you would like to share, visit wakeupmoment.com to tell your story!

Web site: www.wakeupmoment.com
E-mail: lee@wakeuplive.com

Founder and Spiritual Director

Agape International Spiritual Center
Address: Culver City, CA
Web site: www.agapelive.com

Debra J. Berg is an author and speaker to colleges, nonprofits, and corporations. She is an experienced talk show host and guest as well as the executive director of the National Institute of Civic Enterprise (NICE). The NICEnetwork's mission is to assist citizen-inventors who seek to change communities by addressing chronic social problems in the U.S. In addition, Debra is the founder of Power of One Publishing which promotes the successes of these citizen "civic entrepreneurs" through books, media and the Web.

Address: 3326 Site to See Ave. Eustis, Fl. 32726
Telephone: 352-589-5981
Web sites: www.powerone.org & www.debraberg.com
debra@powerone.org

Barry Walter Boyd is a living life mentor, international presenter and an ambassador to the spirit of delight that lives inside of all life. He is the author of ShareandProsper.com, a living success system and Career of Humanity™ which entertains, inspires and assists people around the globe to create their own Living Life Plan and attract the resources to live it.

Address: 4933 W. Craig Rd. #200
Las Vegas, NV 89130
Telephone: 702-325-0502
Web site: www.livinglifeplan.com or www.shareandprosper.com
E-mail: wakeup@livinglifeplan.com

Steve is a #1 best-selling author, a frequent radio and television guest, a highly regarded speaker and writes articles for many leading publications. He is known as "The Business Prophet"™ due to his unique insights and ability to ensure businesses maximize their growth, profitability and valuation. He has led some of the fastest growing companies in America, including the 6th fastest growing small public company in the U.S. (as rated by *Inc. Magazine*).

Managing Principal, Profit Partners Unlimited
CEO, Corporate Toolbelt
Member, Boards of Directors
Web site: www.thebusinessprophet.com
E-mail: steve@thebusinessprophet.com

Helping people assess their lives, create goals, and map out plans to achieve them is the life work and passion of Florence Callender. She is a valued public speaker, inspiring teacher, life strategist, health coach and author. She is a highly sought-after presenter with the unique ability to inform and inspire individuals to pursue their dreams by organizing their lives through understanding how the mind works and directing their thoughts to facilitate living a life of possibilities NOW.

Address: 2013 Chestnut St.
Baldwin, NY 11510
Telephone: 516-377-7490
Web site: www.NewMindNewLife.com
E-mail: info@NewMindNewLife.com

Michael B. Conlon, J.D. is the president of Carolina Parks, LLC, a real estate investment firm with over 600 rental units and property valued at over $23 million. He is the author of *Life Skillz 101: Why the Hare Kicks Tortoise Butt Every Time*, and a personal coach who helps other entrepreneurs and real estate investors achieve their goals.

Telephone: 321-662-8159
E-mail: mconlon1@gmail.com

As the Bay Area's Foremost Photographer, Rochelle is first choice for those seeking creative, intellectual and professional photography with over 30 years experience and a reputation built on integrity, timeliness, customer service and skill. Rochelle has had personal training from some of photography's greats such as Al Weber, Cole Weston, and Brian Taylor. In addition to photography, Rochelle enjoys writing, has worked in the high-tech industry, and is available for speaking engagements. E-mail for your free copy of *Ask the Right Questions: Hiring a Professional Photographer.*

Alter Image Photography
Telephone: Northern California 408-732-2329
Web site: www.rochelleconover.com
E-mail: rochellewakeupabundance@yahoo.com

Mary Gates is a visionary, speaker, author, mentor and spiritual healer. She discovered her calling as a personal transformation facilitator after experiencing miraculous healing from more than 30 years of physical ailments that her doctors told her she could not be cured. Now she lives in vibrant health and is passionate about helping others experience great living, too! Get her free eZine, *Vibrant*, from her Web site.

Open Gates LLC
Telephone: 866-218-5452
Web site: www.opengatesnetwork.org
www.shaklee.net/opengates
E-mail: opengates.us@gmail.com

   John G. Geier, Ph.D., is a prolific author of assessment systems. He is chairman of the board of Geier Learning International and sets the pace for research into human activity. He is internationally recognized for the development of the Universal DISC® Behavioral Model and maintains an alliance with Persolog, GmbH. of Germany.

Geier Learning International
Address: 10650 County Rd. 81, Suite 101
Maple Grove, MN 55369
Telephone: 763-493-3374
Web site: www.geierlearning.com

   Certified General Accountant
   Margaret Good has an accounting practice in Canada and has been working closely with her clients since 1982 as a business coach who helps them to reach their goals and personal potential. She is actively involved in her community and holds various board appointments in organizations that advance the status of women and girls.

Address: Brampton, Ontario, Canada
Telephone: 416-804-0520
E-mail: margaret.good@rogers.com

   Rebecca Grado is a psychotherapist, author and speaker. She is also the clinical supervisor and director at Awakening: A Center for Exploring Living and Dying. She leads numerous groups and workshops in the Bay area on female empowerment and spiritual principals. Rebecca is the co-author of the upcoming book *The Fairest One of All*. Her joy and passion for life inspires others to live life fully every day.

Telephone: 925-829-6745
Web site: www.RebeccaGrado.com
E-mail: RebeccaGrado@att.net

Dan Hanneman is a Licensed Professional Clinical Counselor and Certified Hypnotherapist with combined business and professional backgrounds in metaphysics, religious science, hypnosis, psychology, motivational techniques and personal development systems. He operates a private practice as a hypnotherapist, counselor and spiritual life coach. Dan also inspires and teaches others around the country about living from a place of love, and living out a life from their soul's highest desire.

> Address: 101 N. Virginia Street, Suite 160
> Crystal Lake, IL 60014
> Telephone: 815-788-0471
> Web site: www.danhanneman.com
> E-mail: danhanneman@sbcglobal.net

A sought-after speaker, author and workshop leader, Bill Harris is founder and director of Centerpointe Research Institute and creator of Holosync® audio technology. Started in 1989 with borrowed recording equipment set up on his kitchen table, Centerpointe now has over 150,000 Holosync® users in 172 countries.

> Centerpointe Research Institute
> Address: 1700 NW 167th Pl., Suite 220
> Beaverton, OR 97006
> Telephone: 800-945-2741
> Web site: www.centerpointe.com

Mike is the founder of Take Control Self Defense and was nominated for an Emmy Award for his cable television show, Annual Self-Defense Fundraiser. Since 1988, he has been corporate America's number one women's personal protection and self empowerment trainer. As a seminar leader and keynote speaker, Mike has provided life-saving strategies and techniques to thousands of women with his live events in 20 states, and to over 3.5 million via his television and radio appearances. He has been inspiring and educating women and their daughters for almost two decades.

> Address: 7041 N. Via Nueva St.
> Scottsdale, AZ 85258
> Web site: www.TakeControlSelfDefense.com
> E-mail: Mike@TakeControlSelfDefense.com

Weston was raised primarily in California's Sierra Nevada mountains and went to Stanford for his bachelor, graduate and law degrees. He recently began Cogent Change, a firm that offers coaching and training programs including "Real World Economics" and "Weed Out Fear." He is also the co-founder of MySleepMask, which provides sleep apnea patients both at-home diagnosis and chronic care management.

> Address: 22603 NE 231st Ave.
> Battle Ground, WA 98604
> Telephone: 646-338-1512
> E-mail: Weston@CogentChange.com or Weston@MySleepMask.com

Heissam is an established newspaper publisher, author, college speaker and real estate investor born in Halifax, Nova Scotia and raised in a Lebanese household.

H.J. Communications, Inc.
Address: 14024 St. Leo Ct.
Orlando, FL 32826
Telephone: 407-709-5098
Web site: www.heissamjebailey.com
E-mail: heissam@heissamjebailey.com

Jesse and Melva have been married for over 30 years and have more than 60 years of combined experience as psychotherapists, relationship educators, workshop leaders, public speakers, authors and consultants. They recently authored an inspiring new book, *Mining for the Gold in Your Relationships*, released in June 2007. The book contains a simple, but extremely effective, process capable of transforming the reader's personal life and relationships. The forward for the book was written by best-selling author Harville Hendrix, Ph.D. (*Getting the Love You Want*) and is endorsed by best-selling authors Marianne Williamson (*Return to Love*) and Iyanla Vanzant (*Acts of Faith*).

Address: 29488 Woodward Ave. 329
Royal Oak, MI 48073-0903
Telephone: 248-547-1180

With over 15 years of experience in the fitness industry as a speaker, author, certified trainer and nutritionist, Brian J. Johnston has become know as "The Trainer's Trainer" among fitness professionals. In 1998, he founded EVOLUTIONS Total Wellness to "educate, encourage and equip people to positively influence others." From a passion to speak, teach, and lead, Brian has developed an informative and entertaining series of "secrets" with corporations, colleges and kids. Frustrated by the increasing number of unhealthy statistics, Brian also created the SMART START System: A Common Sense Approach to Personal Fitness Success™. To schedule a personal appointment, coaching session, or speaking event, please contact:

Telephone: 404-451-4170
Web site: www.evolve-now.com
E-mail: info@evolve-now.com

Ganada has been a licensed Nuclear Medicine Technologist since 1991 and remains active in the profession. She has a B.S. in Healthcare Management and an M.A. in Negotiation and Conflict Management from California State University Dominguez Hills. Ganada has completed DRPA training for basic and advanced mediation skills provided by the Los Angeles County Bar Association and has been a volunteer mediator for the Los Angeles Superior Court since 2003.

Alternative Solutions and Peacebuilding (ASAP)
Web site: www.aboutasap.com
E-mail: gkearney@aboutasap.com

Kayli Martin and Donna Lee Cutler have a common philosophical attitude that encourages a conscious choice to play and be joyful in every endeavor they undertake, whether for work or outside of work. They both bring a wealth of creative spirit and positive intent to their efforts. Ms. Martin, M.A., has a passion for assisting others to make choices that change their lives for the better. Her background in philosophy and ethics provides a solid foundation for ensuring the basics are integrated in everything the company offers. Ms. Cutler, B.A., has a wide experience in basic business details and taking creative visualization and imagination through the process of product development. She embraces a personal passion for a variety of business, creative and inspirational expressions.

Chi Whiz Creations
Telephone: 425-827-4830 Fax: 425-889-2504
Web site: www.chiwhizcreations.com
E-mail: kayli@chiwhizcreations.com, donna@chiwhizcreations.com

David Mason is "The Performance Development Coach," a trainer and best-selling author of *Marketing Your Small Business For Big Profits.* David works with people from around the world, one-on-one or in groups, to help them get unstuck, erase frustration, create goals and develop laser focus that allows them to grow both personally and professionally. To have David speak at your next event or for private book signings, e-mail info@DavidMasonSpeaker.com.

Mason Performance Development Inc.
Address: P.O. Box 702
Amherst, NS B4H 4B8
Telephone: 902-660-3070
Web site: www.YourBigProfits.com or www.ItsTimeToGrow.com
E-mail: Dave@MasonPD.com or info@DavidMasonSpeaker.com

Doug McKee is a nurse anesthetist and has been practicing anesthesia for 35 years.
He is the author of Mental Mechanics: A Repair Manual, the first book that explains how humans think. He teaches, counsels and speaks about the internal thought processes involved in knowledge, emotions, needs, wants, values and self-esteem, and how we use our internal thinking processes to relate to the rest of the world.

Address: 133 Country Club, Brownsville, TX 78520
Telephone: (956) 792-5099
Web site: www.mentalmechanic.com
Email: doug@mentalmechanic.com

Mohd, Suria . . . .*Page 81*
Suria is Asia's most-trusted weight loss guru. She is the founder of Shape Watchers Asia, a company that has helped thousands of food lovers in Asia lose weight and keep it off without giving up the food they love. She is an expert weight loss speaker, writer of local weight loss reality television shows, is heard on the radio and has been published in magazines and newspapers.

Shape Watchers Asia
No. 30 Lorong 27 Geylang Citiraya Centre #03-01/02
Singapore 388164
Telephone: +65 6749 7717 Fax: +65 6841 8465
Web site: www.shapewatchersasia.com
E-mail: info@shapewatchersasia.com

Nicolle, Steven . . . .*Page 151*
Steven Nicolle is a certified Sommelier and has held management positions in all restaurant Front of House departments. Also, as a public speaker, Steven gives talks on overcoming fear of change through his own experience and as a life coach helps others achieve their dreams of living happy abundant lives.

Telephone: 519-941-0291 or 888-941-0291
E-mail: ssnicolle@wightman.ca

Pellegrino, Barbara . . . .*Page 71*
From the reefs of Australia to the rainbows of Hawaii, Barbara is a speaker, author and consultant and has traveled the world as the creator and presenter of "Treasure Mapping Your Way to Success," making dreams come true for herself and many others. Barbara began her quest for living the life she loves after studying and teaching "Mind Powers." She studied *Money and You* with Robert Kiyosaki and then earned her certification as a NLP (Neuro-Linguistic Programming) facilitator and trainer. She continues in her quest to bring you the best!

Web site: www.treasuremapyourlife.com
E-mail: Barbara@visionboards.net

Reid, Gregory Scott . . . .*Page 113*
A #1 best-selling author, Gregory Scott Reid has become known for his energy and candor on the speakers' platform and his signature phrase "Always Good!" An experienced entrepreneur in his own right, he has become known as an effective leader, coach, and "The Millionaire Mentor."

Telephone: 877-303-3304
Web site: www.AlwaysGood.com

Robbins, Anthony . . . .*Page 63*
The Anthony Robbins Foundation is a non-profit organization created to empower individuals and organizations to make a significant difference in the quality of life for people who are often forgotten—youth, homeless and hungry, prisoners, elderly and disabled. Our international coalition of caring volunteers provides the vision, the inspiration, the finest resources and the specific strategies needed to empower these important members of our society.

Telephone: 800-554-0619 or 858-535-6295
Web site: www.anthonyrobbinsfoundation.org
E-mail: foundation@anthonyrobbinsfoundation.org

Clinical Hypnotherapist, Reiki Master Teacher, International Speech Competition first place winner and mother. Gail A. Sinclair is a former anorexic who teaches women to not let their bodies get in the way of their lives, by addressing negative body image issues and eating disorders. She offers teleseminars, podcasts, workshops, coaching and her unique "I AM" process to return women to a moment when they loved their bodies.

Steps to Manage
Telephone: 503-473-2690
Web site: www.stepstomanage.com
E-mail: gail@stepstomanage.com

Kay is the author of *Point of Power: A Relationship With Your Soul and Wheel of Life Cycles: The Power of Love to Heal Your Life*. She also co-authors with English astrologer Margaret Koolman in the book *Gateways to the Soul:Heart of Astrology*, to be published in 2007.

Global Family Education, Inc.
Address: P.O. Box 60
Kapa'a, Kau'ai, HI 96746
Telephone: 808-822-4332
E-mail: info@globalfamilyeducation.com

Art Solis was born in El Paso, Texas, on February 2, 1964—Ground Hog Day. Art became a born-again Christian at the age of 19 and received the call to the music ministry in 1980. Today, along with the music ministry, Art loves to write books. His passion is to write books that inspire, teach and help others. Art's goal is to have 100 books published before he dies.

Web site: www.financialheights.com
Email: artsolis7505@yahoo.com

"Helping loving people like you create a life of passion and abundance!"
Jase is a coach, speaker, hypnotist and entertainer specializing in persuasion training, mastery of fear and success training. Would you like to have Jase speak to your group for free? To find out how you can now book Jase to speak to your group or present his comedy hypnosis show for free, please visit call, e-mail him, or visit his Web site.

Life Tigers Seminars
Telephone: 866-780-8183
Web site: www.lifetigers.com
E-mail: info@lifetigers.com

Creator of *Wake Up...Live the Life You Love*. With more than 12 million stories in print, his message is reaching an international audience. Steven E has joined many of his co-authors at seminars and lectures. Some of these authors include Wayne Dyer, Anthony Robbins, Deepak Chopra, Eddie Foy III, Donald Trump University, and many more inspirational souls. He and his Wake Up team are now developing a PBS show that will teach, inspire and touch even more people with his message, "Reject fear and hopelessness in order to seize hope, purpose, and meaning for a more fulfilling life."

Web site: www.wakeuplive.com

Living in Abundance

Ben Sutter has a diverse background in farming, business and trading in the markets. His passion—helping people find their ideal life through the book *The Passion Test* and other personal growth strategies—drives him to write and speak on the subject. Ben is living proof that challenges and limitations can be overcome by focusing on the desired positive outcome. Look for Ben's book on passionate living.

A Prosperous Spirit
Address: 43299 170th St.
Morristown, MN 55052
Telephone: 507-351-0360
Web site: www.aprosperousspirit.com
E-mail: info@aprosperousspirit.com

Jay Westbrook is an award winning clinician, author, speaker and nationally recognized expert on end-of-life issues. He is clinical director of a hospital's Palliative Care Service and clinical director of his own company, Compassionate Journey: An End-of-Life Education and Consulting Service. Westbrook is an amazing speaker who powerfully presents the transformative aspects of suffering.

Compassionate Journey
Telephone: 818-773-3700
Web site: www.CompassionateJourney.com

LaTanya White is a Master Mixologist and owner of 71 Proof, LLC, a spirits industry professional services enterprise which proudly serves responsible adult drinkers in the northern Florida and southern Georgia areas. The services offered by 71 Proof include bar catering, bar consulting, bar training and Custom Cocktail Developmentsm. She received her training in bartending and mixology from American Bartending School located in Tampa, Florida in July 2006. LaTanya was recently featured in the April 2007 issue of *Essence Magazine* as "The Side Hustle of the Month," and is currently one of Tallahassee's "Women to Watch," according to *Tallahassee Woman* magazine. She can be reached through email for mixology advice or suggestions.
E-mail: latanya@71ProofLLC.com

Christy is the author of five books, including her bestselling book *Perfect Pictures* (GMA Publishing), which focuses on releasing the expectation that one be perfect. Christy is also a captivating and dynamic speaker. She consistently speaks in front of large groups on the topics of how to bust perfect pictures, the Law of Attraction, suicide prevention and how to heal after someone commits suicide. She is also a certified Light Body instructor and Law of Attraction coach.

Personal Empowerment
Address: 64 E. Uwchlan Ave. #107
Exton, PA 19341
Telephone: 610-883-7345
Web site: www.christywhitman.com
www.7essentiallaws.com
E-mail: Christy@christywhitman.com

Karen works with our three main consciousness centers: the head, heart and hara. She leads people to discover intuitive whole-body listening to create successful personal and professional relationships.

Telephone: 480-998-8455
Web site: www.HeartOfCourage.com

Kerron "Ron" Wilson is the owner of a well-recognized mortgage and investment firm that is based in South Florida. He is also a certified national trainer with BOWA (Bert Oliva Wealth Academy) where he conducts numerous workshops, seminars and speaking engagements on leadership, motivation, character development, goal setting, corporate strategies, sales techniques, body language (non-verbal communication) and "humanology" (the power of human potential).

Address: PO Box 770487 Coral Sprints, Fl. 33077
Telephone: (954) 882-7629
Web site: www.kerronwilson.com, www.bertoliva.com
E-mail: info@kerronwilson.com

Ph.D. University of Notre Dame. Theology. Specialties: Bible, Ancient Near East, Early Christianity. Professor, Seton Hall University (1965-2002). Director, Archaeological Expeditions (10) to Tell Safut, Hashemite Kingdom of Jordan (1982-present). Guest lectures in Germany, France, Jordan, Egypt (Nile tour guide) and The People's Republic of China. Post campus activities: Professional speaker, Health & Wellness coaching, real estate, Certified Vacation Specialist.

Web site: GrowRichwithPeaceofMind.com, ReligionStudiesInstitute.com,
WellnessAllAroundUs.com, GrowWealthServices.com, DonBuysProperties.com,
DonSellsproperties.com, GoWhenYouWantTo.com
E-mail: wimmerdh@juno.com or PieceofMindAdvisor@aol.com

Linda is a wife, mother, teacher and spiritual leader. Her passions are spirituality, spiritual direction, music and caring for people. At present she ministers at a Church of Christ, in the suburbs of Melbourne, Australia. Her Heart-Song resonates with justice, equality and acceptance for the world.

Telephone: 61-39-548-2676
Web site: www.deeplyimplicit.com
E-mail: info@deeplyimplicit.com

Barbara Zagata is the chef and proprietor of Santa Barbara Soul Food, Inc., an organic catering company based on teamwork and earth-friendly values. She began teaching children how to cook when asked to volunteer at her son's alternative school. Since then, Barbara has founded Camp Cucina, a culinary crash course for teens, as well as other programs designed to bring families together through inspiring food choices that empower the individual while creating a sense of community. Barbara currently speaks to students on college campuses regarding sustainable food choices, as well as promoting the concept "Relaxing in Abundance Now."

Web site: www.sbsoulfood.com, www.campcucina.com, www.pathway2abundance.com
E-mail: barbara@sbsoulfood.com

WAKE UP...
LIVE THE LIFE YOU LOVE

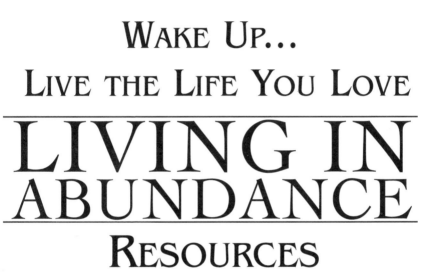

LIVING IN
ABUNDANCE
RESOURCES

RESOURCES

James Malinchak
www.BigMoneySpeaker.com
www.Malinchak.com
www.CollegeSpeakerSuccess.com

James Malinchak is one of America's most requested motivational speakers and has delivered over 2,200 presentations for college and universities, corporations and associations, business gatherings and youth events. Because of his success in the speaking industry, he launched the College Speaking Success Boot Camp and the Big Money Speaker Boot Camp. With these programs, he shows anyone who wants to speak or who is currently speaking how to make $100,000 - $1,000,000+ a year as a professional speaker.

RESOURCES

Early To Rise
866-344-7200
www.EarlyToRise.com

Early To Rise is the Internet's most popular health, wealth and success e-zine. Their purpose is to support their readers in a quest to succeed in life. When you sign up for Early To Rise, you will receive a message in your e-mail inbox every morning, full of good cheer and useful advice; you will be armed with loads of experience, useful insights and great resources.

Early To Rise wants you to succeed in any area of life you wish. They can give you inspiration or show you how it's done. Their goal is to get you to understand something, remember something, realize something and, ultimately, to do something that will make you healthier, wealthier and even wiser every day of the year.

When you read Early To Rise, you will be reminded of all that is possible for you. A better, brighter, fuller, and happier future is at your fingertips. Go to www.EarlyToRise.com to sign up for this free e-zine!

Noetic Pyramid

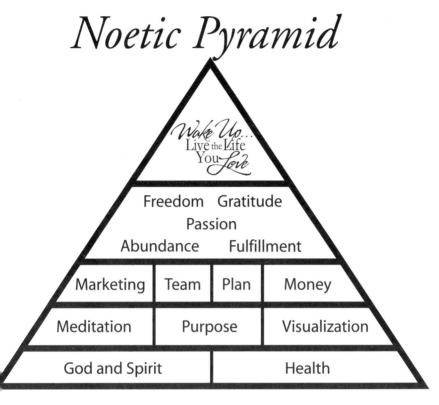

The Noetic Pyramid is a systemic way of looking at the benefits of learning and implementing the attitudes, beliefs and behaviors that must always precede real abundance in life.

With your faith in God and attention to your health as the foundation, learning what we call The 7 Secrets of Living the Life You Love is easier and has much more meaning.

Then we must develop the internal structures of abundance: find your purpose through meditation or prayer, then visualize your desired future.

The Pyramid then leads you from a firm foundation to the external techniques of planning, teamwork, marketing and acquiring the necessary money. None of these external elements will be meaningful without the foundational elements, but neither will these essential elements inherently lead to abundance.

We must realize the benefits of learning and utilizing the internal structure and external techniques to create abundance, freedom, gratitude and fulfillment so we can truly live the life we love. An abundant life has meaning beyond ourselves, so we must seek to improve the lives of others. When we use our freedom to the benefit of others, when we are thankful for the opportunity to share the blessings of a materially abundant life, then we are fulfilled beyond our ability to imagine.

This is what we want everyone around the world to do: *Wake Up...Live the Life You Love.*

WAKE UP...
LIVE THE LIFE YOU LOVE

LIVING IN
ABUNDANCE

A GIFT FOR YOU

A GIFT FOR YOU

Wake Up…Live the Life You Love wants to give you a gift that will get you moving on the path to personal abundance. Please visit www.wakeupgift.com today and start on your way to Living in Abundance!

NOTES AND PERSONAL REFLECTIONS